Pretty Pet-Friendly

EASY WAYS TO KEEP SPOT'S DIGS STYLISH & SPOTLESS

JULIA SZABO

WILEY

Wiley Publishing, Inc.

Howell Book House
Published by Wiley Publishing, Inc., Hoboken, New Jersey

Photography by Heather Green (www.heathergreenphotography.com)

For general information on our other products and services or to obtain technical support please contact our Customer Care Department within the U.S. at (800) 762-2974, outside the U.S. at (317) 572-3993 or fax (317) 572-4002.

Wiley also publishes its books in a variety of electronic formats. Some content that appears in print may not be available in electronic books. For more information about Wiley products, please visit our web site at www.wiley.com.

Library of Congress Cataloging-in-Publication Data:
Szabo, Julia, 1965-
  Pretty pet-friendly : easy ways to keep Spot's digs stylish & spotless / Julia Szabo.
      p. cm.
  Includes index.
  ISBN 978-0-470-37728-4
1. Pets—Housing. 2. Dogs—Housing. 3. Cats—Housing. 4. House cleaning. 5. Interior decoration. I. Title.

  SF414.2.S93 2009
  636.08'31—dc22
                                    2008046483

Printed in the United States of America

10 9 8 7 6 5 4 3 2 1

Book design by Melissa Auciello-Brogan
Book production by Wiley Publishing, Inc. Composition Services

This book is dedicated to my beautiful brindle bully Britannia, Tige, 1994–2008; my beloved blue Burmese, Ludmilla, 1998–2008; and my artist mother, Martha Szabo, whose paintings of my departed animals conjure them alive.

Table of Contents

Resource Guide 183

Index 208

About the Author

Julia **Szabo** produces and writes the weekly "Pets" column for the *Sunday New York Post*, and the monthly "You & Your Pet" column for *Country Living* magazine. Her writings on pets have also been published in the *New York Times* "T" magazine, the *New Yorker*, *Town & Country, Centurion, Departures, Travel & Leisure, Interview, The American Dog Magazine, The Bark*, and *Traditional Home*. She also blogs for PajamasMedia.com and Ceslie.com. She is the author of several books, including *Animal House Style: Designing a Home to Share with Your Pets*, and a frequent guest of Sirius Satellite Radio's "Morning Living" on the Martha Stewart Channel, where she answers callers' questions live. A Phi Beta Kappa graduate of Vassar College, Julia is a member of the advisory boards of North Shore Animal League America (www .animalleague.org), the world's largest no-kill animal shelter, and The Toby Project, which provides free spay and neuter services to New York City's pets in need (www.tobyproject.org). To reach Julia, e-mail julia@animalhousestyle.com.

Acknowledgments

First, I'd like to express my gratitude to Pam Mourouzis and the rest of the Wiley team for recognizing the need for a book that not only celebrates pets and design with lavish photographs but also explains the down-and-dirty ins, outs, and how-to's of making a home pet-friendly and keeping it that way. Huge thanks to my editor, the talented Tere Stouffer, whose own home is a model of pretty pet-friendliness, and to Kim Fernandez and Betsy Karetnick, scintillating hosts of "Morning Living" on Sirius Radio's Martha Stewart channel—they and their listeners are a wellspring of inspiration and invaluable feedback. A very special thank-you to everyone who so generously contributed images, especially Michael Diver, John Bessler, Dara Foster, Jessica Hegland, Eileen McCarthy, and A. E. Nash, and the patient souls who let me barge into their inner sanctums with my digital camera (hello, Lynda Clark, Charlotte Barnard, and my parents, Martha and George Szabo). How can I ever properly thank the brilliant photographer Heather Green, who trained her unerring lens on her own pretty pet-friendly place, shot the images for the front and back covers, and drafted her entire family into modeling service, as well as Jamie Downey, dynamo publisher of *The American Dog Magazine* and a great friend? For helping keep the "pretty" in pretty pet-friendly, thank you Arsen Gurgov of Louis Licari and Andrea Fairweather of Fairweather Faces. Last, but hardly least, my most heartfelt thanks to the animal shelters and rescue groups across this country that do dog's work every day, tirelessly cleaning and sprucing up to make the atmosphere more inviting for potential adopters—and to the animals of every species and stripe who beautify any space just by their precious presence.

Introduction

> **"** I got a lot of flack when the book came out, from people who thought the subject was silly. **"**

Be careful what you say in an interview, because it could wind up as a quotation on a Web site and come back to haunt you. I made the above statement in a conversation with a fellow journalist about my first book, *Animal House Style*. The quote made it all the way to ThinkExist.com, but it leaves out the rest of what I said: The subject of pets and design—also the subject of this book—is not silly at all.

In fact, for the many pets who languish in animal shelters because house-proud folks hesitate to adopt, fearing that animals mess up a home, design can be a lifesaver. My goal is to encourage more people to visit their local animal shelters and adopt pets—and if that means writing books describing exactly how to keep their homes clean and looking stylish, I'm happy to do it.

I hate to clean and historically have done almost anything to avoid it—unless, of course, I'm on a book deadline, in which case I'll clean like a demon just to avoid writing (please don't tell my editor!). But I love animals and really can't ever see myself living without them. To me, a house isn't a home without at least one pet in residence.

However, living with animals means doing a lot more cleaning than the average petless person. So, just as I've housetrained my pets, I've trained myself to keep an orderly home. I've come to realize that the unconditional love provided by my pets is more than worth a little extra housekeeping effort. Besides loving us no matter who we are or how little money we have, pets lower our blood pressure and help us to lead longer, happier lives. They can alert us to intruders, smoke and fire, or an impending seizure or heart attack; their sensitive noses can even detect cancer.

Entropy is a force of nature—it will mess up your home even if you don't live with pets. So, it's high time to approach housekeeping not as a grind, but as something nice to do for animals in return for all they give us. A little extra housework won't kill you—it will make you stronger, while strengthening the bond between you and your animal companions. The surprising payoff is that your place will look terrific—much better, in fact, than if you lived in a petless residence.

In my younger days, I didn't set great store by decorating my own place, although I could certainly appreciate a well-appointed interior. But reporting on the design-and-décor beat for various newspapers and magazines, and noticing how many chic homes had pets in residence, I quickly discovered how even the most budget-friendly solutions can simplify life with animals, whether you have one dog or several cats.

Nowadays, I'm known for my pet-lifestyle expertise, and I'm a big believer in the importance of keeping pet residences clean and nice-looking. I'm honored that pet lovers all over the country seek out my advice on this subject, and I'm always happy to share what I know and to learn things I didn't know.

You and I love our pets, but for every loved animal in the United States, there are literally thousands more who sit in this country's animal shelters, waiting for a second chance. Sadly, many of them never get that chance. And when disaster strikes—whether it's an act of God, like a hurricane, or something man-made, like the mortgage-foreclosure crisis—thousands more animals wind up homeless. There simply isn't enough space for them all, and many are killed just for lack of cage space.

The overwhelming number of homeless pets in this country keeps me awake nights, and it has motivated me to work closely with my local animal shelter, adopting and fostering pets in need. More important, I do whatever I can to raise awareness of the tremendous rewards of unconditional love that await anyone who goes to a shelter looking to bring home a new best friend. Any time someone stops to admire one of my animals, I give them directions to the city pound, my pets' "alma mater."

Too often, people resist going to an animal shelter because they fear the experience will depress them. Don't be afraid: Go there and give someone a new leash on life. Look at it as your very own extreme-makeover reality show, as you transform a hard-luck stray into a pampered celebrity. My most beautiful, beloved animals are the ones that someone else dumped at an animal shelter. If it were up to me, I'd keep them all; so the ones I couldn't keep myself, I've adopted out to loving new homes.

In rescuing pets and catering to their lifestyle needs, I've found the old saying about "One man's trash . . ." to be absolutely true: Like my pets, some of the most treasured possessions in my home were items of furniture that other people tossed out, and I salvaged out of dumpsters or off the street. After a while, there were so many discarded items that I had to sell or donate many of them after rehabbing them! My favorite is the plant stand I picked up the day before my deadline to turn in this book. It was left on the street with a note that read, "Paint me & I'm beautiful & functional." Substitute the word bathe for paint, and that's the silent message shelter pets are sending us.

You will find that your shelter pet will be much more than a loyal friend: He or she will be your live-in decorator and lifestyle coach, offering free advice on how to arrange your home. My pets taught me everything I know about keeping a pretty, pet-friendly place. They voted with their feet, literally showing me what worked and what didn't. Luckily, I listened—and with this book, I'm just sharing what I was fortunate enough to learn from these natural-born decorators.

If you love animals like I do, you'll agree that no pet should wind up as an animal-shelter statistic, facing a death sentence because he or she chewed some furniture, soiled the house, or dug up the yard. Go out and make the ultimate style statement: Adopt a homeless pet. Every species of animal—from dogs and cats to birds, rabbits, and reptiles—can be adopted instead of purchased. Why create new pets when there are so many out there waiting to love and be loved? I believe animal adoption is the purest, most rewarding form of recycling.

Style is so much more than a silly subject: It can make a serious difference in the world. If you need evidence, check out the various charities that harness the transformative power of

fashion and beauty to help people in tough situations: Soles for Souls, which gathers up donations of footwear, distributing them to people who haven't got shoes, or Locks of Love, which accepts gifts of hair, and then arranges for it to be fabricated into wigs for cancer patients who've lost their tresses to chemo and radiation therapy.

Just as fashion and beauty can help turn people's lives around, design and decorating can make a big difference for needy animals. If each of us keeps a clean, stylish home for our pets, more people will see that adopting a shelter pet does not have to mean saying good-bye to a pretty home atmosphere. In fact, with just a little effort, having a pet-friendly pad can actually mean having the prettiest place on the block. Have fun cleaning and decorating with your best friends!

1

Floor Plan

n a pet residence, the floor is the first and most important consideration. Pets spend a lot of time on the floor; it's our pets' eminent domain. They eat there, sleep there, and play there. Of course, they also make messes there; liquids and solids inevitably go splat on the floor of a pet residence, regardless of how well-behaved the resident pets may be.

Pets also have more feet than we humans do, with each toe ending in a toenail that is so tough, it's actually called a horn. Those horn-nails make contact with the floor a lot, and the effect is similar to having an athlete walk across your floors every day wearing cleats.

Between the scritch-scratch of little paws and the miscellaneous emissions from animals' front and back ends, your floor has to be designed to take a beating—or at least conceal the evidence of heavy scuffing. Like everything else in this book, the high-performance floor also has to be easy to clean (and preferably nonporous) because people who live in pet residences will be swabbing their decks a lot more often than petless folks. Not only does the floor of a pet residence need to wash up with ease, it also needs to withstand the thousands of moppings, polishings, scrubbings, and spot-cleanings it will be subjected to in its lifetime.

That is a tall order. If you're lucky enough to be building a home from the ground up, your floor plan is a blissfully blank slate, and you can call the shots according to what works best for your lifestyle and that of your animals. But if, like most of us, you are buying or renting a place where the floor has already been chosen by someone else, necessity dictates that you live with somebody else's aesthetic choices. In that case, you'll have to work within your budget to modify the existing floor so that it's as pet-friendly as possible.

THRESHOLD OF STYLE

Whether it says WELCOME, GO AWAY, or WIPE YOUR PAWS, a coconut-fiber doormat is the first step to keeping a floor—any floor—looking its best, no matter what it's made of or covered with. These mats are widely available, so it's easy to select one that fits your style and the dimensions of your doorway. Simple and not ornate is best, in my opinion, but for those who wish to express themselves there are any number of colorful, high-style options. Keep in mind that the area surrounding the door mat will require lots of sweeping attention, as coconut fiber "sheds."

POINTS OF ENTRY

To keep a pet residence looking shipshape, it helps to remove one's footwear before entering. At pet residences, where guests are required to remove their shoes before coming inside, interiors are a lot cleaner-looking. However, shoe removal is not always possible when handling multiple large dogs on a snowy winter day, when you're wearing lace-up boots with heavy treads. So the key is creating an entry that can withstand anything pets and people can dish out. Even if redoing all or part of your floor space is not an option, it pays to invest in flooring the high-traffic entry to your home so that it's as impervious to damage as possible—and so that it contains the miscellaneous messes carried in by pets' paws before those messes can contaminate the inner sanctums of your home.

I'm old enough to admit that it's unlikely I'll ever have the means to purchase a plot of land and commission an architect to build me the ultimate dream pet residence. But my consolation is that in compiling this book, I get to consult an architect on the finer points of constructing and decorating a pet-friendly pad. So I—and now you, dear reader—can benefit from the encyclopedic expertise of New York architect Michael Davis on the matter of a pet-friendly entryway, gratis.

"The more impervious the material, the better," Michael explains. "In any home—house or apartment—one should create an entry resistant to dirt where, for example, animals' paws can be cleaned before they are released into the more vulnerable parts of the home. This can be anything from a sealed concrete in a more modern aesthetic, or another cementicious material such as Terrazzo, to stone or ceramic tile.

"Be careful to use a high-performance epoxy grout, and [you] can seal the entire assembly with polyurethane or any number of other sealants, depending upon the material," Michael adds. "Most vendors of tile or stone will provide information about options, which can vary depending upon the material. Typically, granite is far more resistant to staining and scratching than marble. In new construction, this entire area can even be outfitted with a floor drain to facilitate frequent washing, mechanical power-washing (with a high-pressure hose), and/or steam-cleaning."

FLOORING FAUX PAS

Let's start by eliminating the flooring option that should never be used in a pet residence: wall-to-wall broadloom carpeting and wool rugs.

Carpeting

Although advances have been made in terms of making the padding underneath the carpet impervious to liquid damage, it's still a huge time-suck to steam-clean carpeting, and it never does look quite as clean as it does on the day it's installed. It's a fact of life with pets: Whether they've got it coming out the front end or the rear, pets prefer vomiting, urinating, and pooping on soft surfaces. For this reason, soft surfaces, such as carpets, wind up being magnets for pet accidents because animals—understandably—prefer not to have their emissions splashed back at them. Picture a carpeted home with resident parrots; now picture that carpet stained with guano, and you're the one in charge of cleaning the mess. Enough said.

Of course, there are exceptions to this rule; I have met pets who never, ever have accidents on carpeted surfaces. But this is rare. And besides, let's not forget that animals aren't the only ones who leave their mark on carpets: How about kids, guests, and other humans? A floor covering that is easy to clean really is more accommodating and gracious overall. Besides, carpets are notorious dust traps, and dust harbors mites—not good for the well-being of you or your pets. Having carpets also makes housekeeping tougher and more time-consuming, because you have to vacuum extra-diligently to evict all the shedded pet hairs that dig their way deep into the carpet pile. On top of that, the carpet itself sheds, its fibers mingling with pet hairs in such as way as to make the pet hairs that are there look twice as copious.

That being said, there is one useful application for carpeting in a pet residence, but it's not on the floor. I refer to vertical carpeting, the kind that covers cat condos and scratchers. These are very important accessories for house cats, as they permit felines a sanctioned outlet for their instinctive need to strop their claws, which is perfectly normal feline behavior (I am very much against the declawing of cats). Historically, however, cat condo/scratchers have not always been the most attractive additions to a pet residence. In fact, they've been eyesores, often covered in hideous beige broadloom.

Style-conscious people prefer not to display ugly cat-scratchers at home, and the result is that the cats in residence make do with what they find—and that might be your nice furniture or your leather shoes. Sadly, many cats wind up at animal shelters because they mistook people's prized possessions for a sanctioned scratching surface. But happily, more companies are taking style and function into consideration when designing these important pieces of kitty furniture. Nowadays, they're no longer eyesores, thanks to attractive colors and natural materials that don't look out of place in a stylish pet residence. And that means more cats are given outlets for their natural instinct to scratch—and fewer are ending up abandoned at animal shelters. (For wall-mounted vertical cat-scratching options, see chapter 2.)

Wool Rugs

Wool rugs are likewise not a good choice for a pet residence. Like carpets, rugs are pet-emission magnets, and they also make cozy camp sites for dust mites. Plus, because they're not fastened to the floor, rugs can morph into sliding surfboards if there's a large, playful dog or two in the house. If a dog riding a magical sliding carpet collides into, say, a table with knickknacks on it, you've got the ingredients of a spectacular mess—and an epic cleanup operation.

One compromise is to have natural-fiber rugs made of sisal, sea grass, or jute. These rugs look very attractive in any style of décor, will stay in place if they come with a rubberized backing, and are relatively easy to clean (by shampooing and hosing them down outdoors).

By reporting on pet residences, not to mention creating them and living in them myself, I've learned an important house rule: Pet lovers make their own house rules. Besides, architect Michael Davis points out the advantage of antique wool rugs: "Antique, vegetable-dyed rugs are actually much more resistant to staining than newly made chemical-dye carpets, due to the lanolin concentrated in the wool and the ability of the vegetable dye to resist moisture during cleaning." The only downside is that the lanolin in a wool rug makes it smell like, well,

L.A. Confidential

I once stayed overnight in the Santa Monica home of an Oscar-winning actress who had not one, but two, houses on her picturesque property, located a short walk (a few dozen yards) away from each other. One of the houses, the newer one, was sun-drenched, with perfectly pet-friendly floors covered throughout in attractive tiles. The other house, an older, more nondescript structure, was dark and carpeted wall to wall in drab nylon broadloom. Can you guess where the actress's several large dogs lived?

Shockingly, she kept her "rescued" dogs in the older, carpeted house, where there was ample evidence that she'd left the dogs home alone for many hours at a time with no one to relieve them, and the poor creatures had to do what came naturally—all over the carpet. The actress didn't want her pristine new house to be "messed up" by the dogs, so she consigned them where the sun didn't shine—when in fact letting them live with her in sun-filled, tile-floored splendor would have been the decoratively correct thing to do (not to mention more humane). Ah, the irony of it all.

I think about those dogs often and how much easier and more pleasant their lives, and that of their owner, would be had she made the right flooring choice for her pets. It's easy for otherwise extremely intelligent people to forget common sense and make a mistake like this.

like a sheep. Dogs are descendants of the wolf, after all—a natural predator of the sheep—and have been known to urinate on lanolin-rich rugs by way of marking their territory. (No kidding: I've seen my own dogs do this, which is one reason I forwent antique rugs.)

However, if you love woolen or antique rugs too much to live without one, and you anchor your floor art with a substantial piece of furniture such as a sofa and/or table—and you don't mind that you'll be doing a lot of spot-cleaning (more on that topic in chapter 7) and vacuum cleaning (more on that in chapter 6) to keep it looking its best, by all means go ahead and lay down a wool rug or two in your pet residence.

The payoff for all that extra cleanup is seeing your pets luxuriating on the rug, stretching themselves out, and rolling around to give themselves a back rub! Pets do love making themselves at home on a nice, cozy rug, and as animal lovers, we love doing what we can to make them feel right at home; it can be very entertaining to watch! Just please don't get one of those antique hooked rugs. Unless you hang it high on your wall, it will be destroyed by your pets' nails in no time flat.

FLOORING THAT WORKS

Your choice of flooring can make or break a happy pet lifestyle. Maintaining a pleasant home atmosphere can be easy and hassle-free—or it can be a constant, grinding chore. It's really your choice. Since I prefer to opt for hassle-free, that's the goal of all the advice offered in this book, specifically in the following sections.

Modular Carpet Tile: Accent the "Pet" in Carpet

Modular carpet tile is a brilliant choice for a pet residence. It has a low-tack adhesive, so it won't damage your existing floor. In fact, it can help prolong a wood floor's life by acting as a protective barrier against mess and, more important, sound. This is especially important if, say, you live in an apartment building, on any floor higher than ground level, where the footfalls of you and your pets are magnified in stereophonic sound to the irritation of your downstairs neighbors (who then lodge complaints with your landlord and . . . you get the idea: This scenario is to be avoided at all costs).

High-quality carpet tiles come in an array of materials, colors, and patterns so impressive that even decorators are excited about them. But the best thing about modular carpet tile is how inexpensive it is. If an accident occurs, whether the culprit is a human or an animal, you can quickly lift up the tile and give it a good washing. If that doesn't work, you can toss the tile without feeling too badly about it; not only was it created from recycled materials, but it's also inexpensive enough that it doesn't feel like a huge, sinful waste. And if you're handy with a carpet cutter, you can scallop or otherwise carve the edges, and use your customized tiles to create all sorts of fun designs on your floor. Customizing carpet tiles happens to be one of designer and DIY guru Todd Oldham's trade secrets, as described in his book *Handmade Modern*.

Modular carpet tile can also be used to enhance what I call "critter comfort" in a pet residence. As a general rule, pets love hanging out on a carpeted surface. (Think about it: Would you want to lie down on the bare, hard floor?) Because our pets love to follow us around and lie down near us, it's a nice idea to use carpet tiles to create a stylish, practical reclining area for a dog or cat near a favorite human hangout, such as a desk or the TV. For senior pets who suffer from arthritis, carpet tiles can be a stylish way to make the floor a safer, more comfy place so that old friends won't slip and hurt themselves.

Carpet tiles can also be used judiciously to designate what I call "no-paw zones." At the New York home of designer Kevin Dresser and Kate Johnson, Roebling the rabbit—a.k.a. Brooklyn Bunny—loves scampering along what the designers have dubbed "The Brooklyn Bunway": a pathway made out of customized carpet tiles. Rabbits love to nibble on whatever you've got, but anything made of wood has special appeal. However, slipping around on a wood floor does not appeal to Roebling the rabbit. So, to preserve the longevity of their vintage wood furnishings, Kevin and Kate ingeniously laid down the Bunway in the part of their loft that has no wood furniture. That way, Roebling has freedom to romp on the carpeted areas he prefers, and Kevin and Kate's wood furniture stays safe from harm. Now that's what I call creative!

The same aesthetic logic can also be applied to cats. Sure, your cat has a carpeted condo/ scratcher—but there are times when a limber feline likes to flex her claws horizontally as well as vertically. With that in mind, carpet tiles made of coconut fiber may be placed at strategic points around a pet residence, especially one with wood floors, to give cats a sanctioned scratching option that's horizontal, so they won't tear up the floor as if it were a tree trunk.

To make sure Kitty knows what's okay to scratch, sprinkle some fragrant catnip on the coconut-fiber carpet tiles, and that's where she'll leave her mark. Use organic catnip—it has a stronger aroma—and rub the leaves together with your fingers to release that irresistible aroma before scattering them.

Knock on Wood

Natural wood is a traditional flooring option that almost everyone loves, which explains why so many makers of synthetic flooring strive to achieve the "look of wood" in their products. I'll turn the floor over to architect Michael Davis: "When it comes to wood, harder is better," he says. "Common hardwoods used for interior floors include oak, mahogany, and chestnut, while the most common softwood is pine. These, too, should all be sealed with a polyurethane sealer. [You] can also use exterior-grade wood more resistant to moisture, such as teak, although this and all other woods should be LEED-certified [and] sustainably harvested whenever possible."

Like New Again

One reason hardwoods are preferred for pet residences is that after a few years, once the planks have become extremely dinged and scratched, they can be sanded and/or screened and refinished to look almost as good as new. On the other hand, as Michael Davis explains, "Engineered flooring typically provides a thin veneer of the finish material, which cannot be sanded more than once or twice." In other words, if you want to take your floor back to a like-new look, you'll need to replace the entire thing. Therefore, it's far better to start off with durable, natural hardwoods so that you have the option of sanding at a later time.

How long your wood floors can go without being sanded depends on the size and activity level of your pets. Large or giant dogs obviously carry more weight, which means their nails will put more stress on the floors by hammering them every day. Smaller dogs and cats, on the other hand, won't put as much stress on a wood floor—as long as their nails are clipped short. The size of your pet should also dictate what color floor you choose. If you have large dogs, steer away from very dark finishes—these are tough to keep looking their best, as traffic from pets and people has a way of leaving its mark. The best choice of finish is anything on the light side, such as oak, which reveals fewer scratches.

Paint on the Floor

House painters take pains to cover wood floors with drop cloths when rolling paint onto the walls of a room, but paint can also be applied to the floor to give a room pizzazz. Tough, durable deck paint in white makes a room feel bigger, as I learned when I painted my kitchen floor white. Plus, if you've got a less-than-perfectly housetrained dog, a white-painted floor helps a great deal to locate accidents in the early-morning hours while you're still sleep-walking, so you can clean the mess up quickly, before it has a chance to sink into the wood. A coating of paint also helps protect and spruce up a wood floor that's somewhat the worse for wear. If you have the patience, consider a decorative paint job for your floor

with, say, a stenciled pattern around the edges of the room, where floors and walls meet, or an allover checkerboard or diamond harlequin pattern of white and black, or white combined with any cheerful contrast color you choose.

Bamboo

Some people just can't live without wood floors—or at least the look of wood floors. Happily for pet residences, that elegant look can be achieved with materials other than wood. One is bamboo, a durable and renewable resource that looks lovely on the floor. For a material that grows in tropical climates, bamboo also stays cool to the touch—a blessing for owners of dogs

Pretty Pet-Friendly

with full, heavy coats. The best brand for pet residences is Teragren, which features an eco-friendly, water-based, and solvent-free finish that may be recoated or resanded as necessary, if the scratches from pets' nails become too prevalent or noticeable.

The Tile File

Ceramic tile is the ideal option for large surfaces in any pet residence. The perfect marriage of form and function, tile is nonporous, easy to keep clean, and looks great. Our pets' body temperature is naturally higher than ours, averaging around 101 degrees Fahrenheit, so the fact that tile is nice and cool to the touch is a big plus for keeping hot-blooded animals comfortable indoors, especially in warm climates. Tile is especially appreciated by dog breeds that get hot under the collar and pant pitiably indoors, even in the dead of winter—think Saint Bernards and Bulldogs—because tile stays cool and keeps a hot dog from having a meltdown.

Aesthetically speaking, your options are not limited to boring, black-or-white subway tile. So, if you're concerned that tiling your floors means walking on boring colors and textures, have no worries: There's a color and shape of tile for every taste and budget. Thanks to contemporary tile artistry, ceramic can mimic almost any decorative material, including slate, wood, or metal (with shades like silver, gold, steel, bronze, and copper)—even leather and sisal!

Meanwhile, stone tile is exceptionally beautiful, durable, and cool to the touch (if expensive). Glass tile is great-looking and helps lighten a dark room by reflecting and maximizing all available light. Another intriguing option is cork tile, which feels wonderful underfoot and comes "pre-dinged" by virtue of this renewable material's character. A waterproof seal makes naturally porous cork nonporous. As for textured versus smooth floor surfaces, it's a toss-up: Smooth will be easy to care for but slippery, especially when wet, while textured will be harder to clean but easier for pets to walk on.

Styles in Tile

Here's a handy glossary so you can sound like a pro when shopping for tiles for your pet residence:

- **Subway tile**   Usually refers to the size 3 inches × 6 inches.
- **Field tile**   Most common sizes are 12 inches square and 12 inches × 24 inches, but field tile can also come in many different dimensions, including 4 inches square, 4 inches × 6 inches, and 6 inches square.
- **Spa size**   Usually refers to larger-size tiles, such as 14 inches × 20 inches.
- **Mosaics**   Come in a variety of custom shapes and sizes, including circular (i.e., "penny") and leaf shapes.

Great Grout

Whatever tile style you choose, and whatever size, from small, round penny tile to 12-inch-square field tile, be sure to give equal attention to the grout used to connect the tiles. Porous grout soaks up liquids, becoming stained and malodorous—thereby undermining the whole point of tile, which is to have a totally nonporous floor surface. Pet residences require nonporous epoxy grout in a shade that is close to the color of the tile (or, if you're doing a mosaic with different colors, select one tile color to key the grout to). Let common sense be your guide: Bright-white grout next to blue glass penny tiles looks smashing, but if you're using earth-toned terra cotta tile, white totally spoils the effect.

Concrete Flooring

If you think of tile in carpet terms, as a modular nonporous floor covering, then a poured concrete floor that is sealed is the equivalent of broadloom: a seamless stretch of nonporous flooring with which to ground your "roomscape" (I just love using that word). Of course, to make concrete nonporous, it needs to be glazed. Not everyone loves the industrial-strength look—a glazed concrete floor certainly wouldn't be a traditionalist's first choice of flooring— but it is one of the most functional floorings for a pet residence.

For a nonporous floor option that's more transitional—meaning it can look at home in many different styles of décor—there's terrazzo, which is essentially concrete with marble chips mixed in, for an elegant faux-marble look that is durable and easy to care for. In either case, for your own comfort and that of your pets, you'll want to have rubber antifatigue matting at key points, notably in the kitchen, where you'll be doing a lot of standing as you prepare meals for your pets and the rest of your family. However, many people and pets are allergic to latex, and latex allergies can develop even in the nonallergic after repeated exposure, so it's safest to use matting made of natural gum rubber instead of man-made latex. Rubber flooring is also excellent for the comfort and sure footing of senior pets whose legs may be a bit wobbly, as it's naturally slip-resistant.

Linoleum and Vinyl

Linoleum, the nineteenth-century invention of Englishman Frederick Walton, continues to be widely used all over the world as a popular sheet flooring material because it's durable (enough to be used on battleships!) and easy to clean. Linoleum is very resistant to heavy foot and paw traffic, and hardens with exposure to air, which only increases its durability. This all-natural, environmentally friendly material has been eclipsed in recent decades by vinyl flooring, and is often confused with it. But the two are not the same: Vinyl, short for polyvinyl chloride, is known to give off toxic VOCs (volatile organic compounds). As a result of rising awareness of VOCs, many chemical-sensitive people are rediscovering the virtues of linoleum for themselves and their families, including the family pets.

Until recently, vinyl flooring was just plain hideous to look at, with a dimpled texture that made cleanup extra-difficult. Thankfully, today's vinyl comes in a range of vibrant colors, whether smooth or embossed in a way that's easier to clean, such as styles that mimic steel diamond plating or penny tiles. The advantage of an embossed vinyl floor is that it's slip-resistant, which is a form of accident insurance for arthritic pets. More good news for pets with joint problems: There's even vinyl flooring that is padded for animals' maximum comfort when walking or lying down.

Available colors and patterns in vinyl are very high style, whether it's a glamorous white that shimmers with metallic accents (great for reflecting available light) or an imitation wood planking that convinces the toughest customer into believing it's really wood grain. And in a creative solution that combines the best virtues of vinyl, wood, and a rug, there are vinyl area mats with the look of wood grain—just the thing to put underneath a cat's litter box, if it's located in a room with a wood floor.

Just as ceramic tile keeps hot dogs cool, vinyl and rubber flooring keeps pets warm—but that's great news if you happen to live with lean, short-coated breeds such as the Chihuahua, Italian Greyhound, or Chinese Crested, who get cold easily. For those concerned about the VOCs in vinyl flooring—and it's a very real concern—there are brands that reduce VOC emissions by 80 to 90 percent. Regardless of what type of vinyl is used, the floor covering should be unrolled and permitted to outgas off-site for a few weeks prior to being installed in a pet residence, especially one with birds. (For more precautions to take when living with birds, see chapter 9.)

FENG SHUI FOR FIDO

The ancient art of aligning and energizing the home can have tremendous benefits for our pets and us. No longer "alternative," the Eastern healing arts are gaining widespread acceptance in America, with acupuncture, Chinese herbal remedies, and plant-based medicines becoming more and more recognized as powerful treatment options for pets as well as people. As you plot the floor plan of your pet residence, now would be a good time to explore feng shui (if you haven't already), the ancient Chinese science of achieving a balanced flow of chi, which is the vital energy force that animates all things.

Like many Eastern practices, feng shui has gained credibility throughout the West for its proven ability to enhance human health and prosperity. In Los Angeles, Dr. Stacy Fuchino, VMD, a.k.a. "the East-Meets-West Vet," incorporates feng shui in his veterinary practice. "I integrate Eastern and Western veterinary medicine, to explore that intermediate area where we can achieve optimal pet wellness," Dr. Fuchino explains. "There's more to medicine than what we have in the Western world. Feng shui is very helpful because it deals with the science of the environment and how it relates to living things."

According to Dr. Fuchino, maintaining neatness is the simplest way to improve chi. "Remove clutter and do not block pathways," he advises. "There should be smooth movement throughout the house at all times." In the world of dog training, behaviorists speak of "corrections" that modify a pet's behavior to be more compatible with our lifestyle. With feng shui, corrections are made to the home—the pet's environment—by means of layout, color, and material selection, as well as placement of furniture and other home accessories.

These adjustments, whether large or small, help to improve the flow of *chi* ("energy") in our environment. And that improved energy flow, in turn, positively affects the energy flow in our pets' bodies, resulting in improved wellness and better relationships between our pets and us. Feng shui also works to pinpoint *sha* ("bad elements") in a dog's environment (i.e., clutter, blocked pathways), correcting anything that could be detrimental to balanced energy flow and creating optimal alignment of Spot's accessories, both the ones he wears on his body (collars, harnesses, and leashes) and the ones that decorate his environment (beds, bowls, toys, and so forth).

Adequate light is key to well-being in a pet residence. "Dimly lit areas are not always best—pets need the energy of light and sun," Dr. Fuchino says. "If a pet is sluggish, he needs to be moved to areas that have more [natural light and] energy." If your place doesn't have much light, try to make use of full-spectrum lightbulbs.

Studies show that spending time with pets lowers blood pressure in humans. If they are more relaxed, we will be too. By harnessing the power of feng shui to make the layout of our pets' digs more conducive to quality togetherness, we improve our own wellness, because the animals will be drawn to hang out with us more. And for those of us who love animals, that's the best floor plan of all.

THE FLOOR AS A BOX SPRING

The floor of a pet residence is where you'll find comfy beds for dogs and cats that look like so many minimattresses sitting on the floor. When it comes to providing nesting spots for beloved beasts, most animal lovers can't stop at just one pet bed. Dog and cat beds come in every imaginable shape and style, and they're covered in a wide range of fabrics to suit any décor (for more on that topic, see chapter 3). But almost more important than what a pet bed looks and feels like is where it's positioned.

Pet bed placement can make the difference between a good night's sleep for Spot—and a restless, fitful string of nightmares that cause him to twitch and cry out in his sleep. Determining where your best friend sleeps is just as important as what he sleeps on, says Dr. Fuchino. "A pet's sleeping area should not be in high-traffic areas of the home," explains the vet, "and pets should not sleep in the bathroom or kitchen. To promote restful sleep, place your pet's bed away from doors or other passageways," he adds. "Otherwise, the constant disruption of sleep could result in health and behavioral issues, such as separation anxiety."

Pretty Pet-Friendly

LITTER LOGIC

Living with cats requires the frequent installation of a special breed of "floor covering": the material that fills Fluffy's litter pan and absorbs her daily droppings. If you already live with cats, then you know how very sensitive this subject is. Cats can be tough customers, and if they don't like the way a particular kind of litter feels under their paws as they walk on it, they won't use the pan—they'll grab your attention by eliminating in inappropriate places as a means of protest.

So, just as we strive to select flooring options that make life easier for our pets and ourselves, we need to apply the same logic to cat litter. The goal is to avoid extra cleanup by selecting high-performance litter. Of course, the exact litter brand you'll end up using is entirely up to your cat. These remarkably discerning creatures vote with their feet, *litter*-ally, letting us mere humans know whether or not the litter arrangement we've made has the right texture. What works well for one pet residence might be disastrous in another, however. (For more on that topic, see chapter 6.)

Personally, I like to use litter brands made of nontoxic, biodegradable ingredients such as corn or wheat. They clump, so they make the chore of scooping go easier and faster, and they don't produce the fine silica dust that's a feature of other clumping litters, which many pets and people find extremely irritating. Plus, aesthetically speaking, they are the litter equivalent of natural-fiber rugs and floor mats, with subtle earth tones that don't call too much attention to themselves in one's décor.

Statistics show that the cat—not the dog!—is the most popular pet in America. We've come a long way since the feline was deified in ancient Egypt for protecting grain from marauding rodents. Nowadays, we spend millions spilling grain for our cats' convenience, in the form of corn and wheat litter! The reason there are more pet cats on record than pet dogs (and tons of litter) is simple: Most cat owners keep more than one cat. If that describes you, remember to avoid extra cleanup by sticking to the litter pan rule: At all times, make available at least one pan per cat, and preferably two.

2

Off the Wall

Walls are a tremendous untapped resource in a pet residence. Too often, what with beds, ramps, bowls, feeders, scratching posts, and the occasional training crate, living with pets reduces the available floor space. Thank goodness for cats, creatures we can look up to, instead of looking down at the floor.

Felines are arboreal by nature, which means they feel at home up high, as in trees. By always climbing to the tallest available perch in a home, looking for all the world like small tigers in tree branches, cats remind us to keep our eyes aimed high. So whether or not you have cats, it's time for you to see walls as blank vertical canvases that can provide a wonderful decorative outlet—and ones that (happily, if you're living in a small space) help maximize what little room you've got.

When I wrote my first book, *Animal House Style*, in 2001, there were no aesthetic options for cat lovers to maximize their wall space: no suitably stylish wall-mounted shelves or scratchers; none at all. (Today, happily, there are plenty.) So I had to devise something myself. My apartment has narrow rooms and very high ceilings—eleven feet high, to be precise. Those long vertical stretches of wall got pretty boring after a while, so I started scheming to jazz them up, while at the same time making them as cat-friendly as I possibly could.

My first step was to ditch the dull white walls I inherited from the apartment's previous tenant. White starts to go gray very quickly in a pet residence—and it's not pretty when it does. A vibrant color—or even a pastel—is much more appealing, not to mention forgiving of scratches and stains. You won't need to touch up colored walls nearly as often as you would with white walls. And if you're lucky enough to have original moldings, it's fun to paint those a different color (even if that color is white) for contrast.

COLOR WAYS

Too many people are timid, if not terrified, when it comes to experimenting with anything bolder than off-white. But I hope living with pets makes you want to take a daring leap into the color field, choosing a hue you like—not one you think is "correct." As a starting point, why not take a cue from the colors of your pets? A bluish gray dog's coat might inspire you to select a lighter shade of the same blue-gray for your walls or your trim; a cat's absinthe-colored eyes might motivate you to try a pale electric yellow-green; a bird's plumage might occasion a pale coral hue, and a rabbit's ear might lead you to paint a room a pretty pink.

In my apartment, the walls are the color of a light tan dog's coat. I've found that this neutral shade goes splendidly with just about everything in my home, from the furnishings to the pets themselves! The tan walls combine with the white-painted moldings to make the experience of coming home feel like walking into a butter-cream-frosted mocha cake. A neutral such as this works well whether your decorating style is traditional, modern, or eclectic.

I once gave a lecture on pretty pet-friendly décor to a terrific, engaged crowd in Cape Cod, Massachusetts; the beneficiary of ticket sales was the excellent Massachusetts SPCA, which operates seven shelters throughout the state, plus the prestigious Angell Animal Medical Centers in Boston and on Nantucket Island. Being my kind of crowd—which is to say, hard-core animal lovers who'd adopted their beloved pets from MSPCA—the audience went along with everything

I said. But they firmly drew the line when I urged them to be bold with paint colors. "We live in Cape Cod homes," one woman explained, meaning there are correct and incorrect colors, and one simply didn't use the incorrect ones when decorating a traditional house on the Cape.

But I say you can be bold with colors, even in a historically traditional setting—all it takes is going just one or two shades darker than you originally intended. So, instead of the palest, anemic yellow, select one that looks more like the yolk of a hard-cooked egg. Even there in Cape Cod, I got a few reluctantly approving nods when I passed around some paint chips, which clearly demonstrated how lovely—and, yes, traditional—the slightly bolder shades really could be. So please be creative, not careful, with color.

Paint Job

Paint is an easy, impactful way to make a style statement in a pet residence, or to freshen up its look without investing too much time or money. However, there are a few house rules to keep in mind when selecting the paint finish that will look best for the longest amount of time. Flat paint is a "don't" in a pet residence—it cannot be wiped without leaving a scar on your wall. Instead, go with a finish that's easily wiped down with a wet sponge, such as eggshell or satin. Semi-gloss is super easy to wipe clean, but decorators advise its use only in kitchens and bathrooms, as it's way too shiny for other rooms in the home, and throws any flaws in your plaster into high relief (not desirable at all if you're planning to have your place photographed for, say, *Metropolitan Home* magazine).

In addition, I would say that semi-gloss paint has one more useful application in a pet residence: in the entryway to your home, where on a rainy day a lot of moisture and mud can get flung on the walls. When my large dogs return from an outing on a rainy day, they (like all dogs) love to shake their bodies vigorously to start the process of feeling comfortably dry again—and the result can make the walls near the front door look like a dingy shower stall! So I've found it helps a great deal to have that easily wipeable semi-gloss finish in this part of my pet residence.

Where you should be careful is in the brand of paint you use, because most ordinary paints are quite toxic. The smell of a freshly painted room is so strong that it's really not possible to spend the night in it; even after it's painted, there's always a fine film of dust on absolutely everything. But did you know that up to 50 percent of the toxic gases (VOCs, short for volatile organic compounds) and carcinogens from traditional paints leak into your home up to six years *after* it has dried on the wall? Until very recently, a few companies offered low-VOC paint, but these formulations were not available in the brightest shades on the color spectrum. Yes, they were an improvement in that they contained fewer VOCs than traditional paint, but they still contributed to poor air quality in the home by outgassing.

Now, happily, there's wonderful Mythic Paint, a company owned by a serious animal lover who shares his home with birds, dogs, cats, and fish. This paint contains zero toxins, zero carcinogens, and zero VOCs, so it's safe to roll on the walls even with pets in the room. The colors are gorgeous and vibrant, and best of all, the company's Web site acknowledges pets as valued family members—which we all agree they are, but not all businesses are bold enough to state their position on the issue so emphatically. (Bravo, Mythic Paint.) But most important, this paint is eight times more durable than paint with VOCs, so your paint job will last longer. It makes complete sense: Volatile paint isn't stable, but a paint containing no volatile ingredients is. Brilliant!

Wallpaper: Writing on the Wall

My foray into fierce paint color would later embolden me to take an even braver creative leap with patterned wallpaper. I'd previously feared that a busy pattern on my walls would drive

me crazy, but I've lived with patterned paper in my parlor for a few years now, and it's actually quite fun. Maybe that's because the pattern I selected happens to be "Adopt Me" by Tyler Hall, which features renderings of actual shelter mutts and excerpts from my last book, *The Underdog.* In my bathroom, meanwhile, the walls are decorated with Tyler Hall's "Cruisin'," which sports images of dogs riding in vintage cars; one of the models happens to be my sweet pit bull Pepper.

If you're selecting wallpaper as a wall-covering option and you have cats, steer away from textured designs, as these will invite inappropriate scratching and clawing.

Decorative painting is a dying art that happily is still practiced by a few talented artisans. In 2002, I was very lucky to have a world-class decorative painter apply his artistry to the walls of my tiny country cottage, as part of a makeover organized by *Traditional Home* magazine

Two views of the entry to my country cottage, where the walls bring the outdoors in thanks to the artistry of Swedish decorative painter Robert Persson. Special thanks to Traditional Home magazine for permitting me to reproduce these images here.

for its *Decorator* supplement. The painter, Robert Persson, lives in Sweden, and one of the homes he'd previously painted happens to be the summer residence of the king and queen of Norway. I was duly impressed, and honored, that my little house would be one of his "canvases."

At my place, Robert used acrylic paint to create a traditional birds-and-flowers pattern in the dining room; and for the tiny entryway, he conjured a floor-to-ceiling tableau of a forest complete with a bushy-tailed squirrel. Over all of his work, from ceiling to floor molding, he laid a coating of oil varnish, to achieve an antique patina that would make the walls look like they'd been that way forever. And at the top of one wall, near the ceiling, he signed his name with pride, adding the name of his hometown, Falun, in "Sverige."

So imagine my horror when, shortly after this extremely special, once-in-a-lifetime paint job and the photo shoot commemorating it was completed, one of my dogs lifted a leg on the wainscoting in the dining room, letting loose a torrent of hot, yellow liquid. I gasped—then practically fell over laughing as I noticed that the urine rolled right off the varnish. The mess wiped up easier than most any spill I've ever had to clean up. Robert's masterpiece was not only extremely pretty, it was pee-proof! (All this, of course, happened before I became enlightened as to VOCs, which oil varnish contains in abundance, but I'll make an exception

You don't have to travel to Scandinavia to find a fine-art muralist. This lovely specimen, "Underwater Mural on Venetian Plaster," was painted by Connecticut artist Melissa Barbieri on the wall of a Massachusetts home.

Pretty Pet-Friendly

Neutering: A Word to the Whizz

Male dogs empty their bladders by lifting their legs (in case you didn't notice), so you'll need to check the bottom foot or so of your wall's height periodically for evidence of inappropriate urination, and wipe or touch up with paint as necessary. In case you've been putting off neutering your male dog or cat, here's some great housekeeping incentive: When neutered males whizz in the house, their urine is much less pungent than that of their intact counterparts. So if Spot whizzes in the house, that pungent odor is tougher to eradicate thanks to all those strong-smelling hormonal ingredients. Plus, it's also lighter in color and therefore leaves behind less staining; intact male urine, on the other hand, is quite viscous and so yellow it's practically orange.

In other species news, neutered rabbits use a litter box, and neutered cats spray less (if at all). Having male animals altered is definitely a giant stride toward making housekeeping easier on you.

in this case, since my pets and I don't live in the country year-round, and since I don't intend to revarnish those walls.)

PANTHER PERCHES

Meanwhile, back in the city, the next step in making my apartment's vertical space fabulously feline-friendly was to establish places for my cats to perch high up along the wall. Collaborating with a carpenter, I devised bracketed demilune (half-circle) shelves made of wood for the enjoyment of my arboreal creatures. Four of these shelves, arranged in a diamond formation on the wall, happen to look dynamite when painted white against a brightly colored wall, adding dimension and architectural interest to what was previously a dull stretch of unused vertical space. But more important, they enable cats to do what cats do best—look down on everybody else!

Many times, I've returned to my place only to wonder where most of the cats might be hiding. Well, it almost always turns out they're not hiding at all—they're lounging around in elevated comfort, enjoying their lofty perches. And when "kitty krazy time" sets in—if you live with cats, you're familiar with that part of the day or night when they enjoy zooming around the room at warp speed, especially if powered by catnip—my cats can zoom upward, leaping from shelf to shelf and getting a fierce workout in the process. All this is seriously entertaining to watch, and keeps my cats from growing fat and bored, a sad fate that befalls too many feline friends.

New cats who have entered my clowder since then, whether fosters or keepers, never take more than a few days to acclimate to the shelves, figuring out how to use the back of my vintage Eero Saarinen sofa—or whatever item of furniture I happen to have backed up to the wall on any given week—as the launch pad to the lowest shelf. Rubbing catnip on the shelves encourages the cats to avail themselves of the vertical playground; so does positioning a catnip toy or meaty treat up there. And once cats decide they like the shelves, it can be tough to get them to come back down. A recent rescue once stayed up there for seven hours straight, happy to accept my offers of food and water but refusing to descend until she was good and ready.

Since repainting the shelves with Mythic Paint, I no longer cringe in dismay when my curious cats lick at them, because the surface is now completely nontoxic. And if someone should deposit a nasty hairball up there that I don't notice for a long time, it's no problem to touch

Shelter Chic

The year 2003 saw the opening of a wonderful cat sanctuary called Tabby's Place. Located in New Jersey, the sanctuary has splendidly colorful rooms created by a professional interior designer expressly for the comfort and amusement of the four-footed residents. Here, cubes—some solid, some configured as cubbies with cutouts for cocooning—are arranged in tiers until they reach the ceiling. With this design, every cat has a pedestal to preen on, and the highly motivated ones may climb their way to the top at their own pace—until they catch the eye of a delighted adopter.

Designer Vanessa von Hessert repurposed one wall of her Manhattan home as a vertical play area for her two cats, Bleaky and Morgan, creating bentwood shelves that resemble the surfboard-inspired work of twentieth-century design giants Charles and Ray Eames. Meanwhile, in Brooklyn, Bill Hilgendorf and Maria Cristina Rueda of Uhuru Design built the ingenious KittyLoft, a set of stairs attached to their wall, for their feline pair, Miles and Athila.

up the spot. I don't even have to evacuate the room; I can keep the cats off the shelf with a plastic sheet, without worrying that they'll inhale anything harmful while the paint dries.

Off the Wall

Craft a Castle for Your Cat

Crafting is all the rage, with crafters hawking their DIY wares on Etsy.com. Here's a project I created for the premiere issue of *CRAFT Magazine:* the Catnip Castle, which transforms ordinary corrugated cardboard into an extraordinary wall-mounted sculpture your feline friend will enjoy climbing and scratching. I envisioned the Catnip Castle as an abstract castle with a tall central tower flanked by a battlement on either side. But the sky's the limit when it comes to design possibilities, so let your imagination be your guide. If your name starts with an M, why not pay homage to animal lover Mary Tyler Moore by making a Catnip Castle in the shape of a super-size M, reminiscent of the one "Mary Richards" had in her apartment?

Time: A weekend
Complexity: Easy

Also, you'll need heavy objects to weigh down glued boards—I used a large piece of plywood, plus several unopened bags of plaster (not shown).

Glue Cardboard Together

Pour carpenter's glue generously onto the center of the first board, and then spread the

Materials and Tools

- Jigsaw
- Glue gun
- Corrugated cardboard pads measuring 36 inches × 48 inches—these are available in bundles of 50 from Uline.com. You only need 35 boards, but it's good to have extra so you can select the most perfect ones.
- Handsaw or reciprocating saw
- $3/8$-inch and $9/32$-inch wood drill bits, 6 inches or longer
- Dried, loose catnip
- Cat treats—Wellness Pure Delights work nicely
- Power drill
- $3/8$-inch washers, 2-inch diameter (4)
- Ratchet with $1/2$-inch socket
- 8 inches × $3/8$-inch lag bolts (4)
- No. 2 pencil
- Carpenter's glue
- Paintbrush, wallpaper brush, and trim guide—for spreading glue; available at paint supply stores.
- Sharp utility/camping knife—I prefer Spyderco.
- Level
- 48-inch rule

glue out with the brush and trim guide. Take care not to pour it on too thick near the edges, or the glue will seep out, leaving unsightly ooze that dries yellow. Lay the next board on top of the glued board, taking care to match up the corners, and repeat until you've attached 10 cardboard pads together. Repeat this process with the next 10 pads. Finally, glue 15 pads together the same way. You now have two cardboard blocks of 10-pad thickness and one of 15-pad thickness.

Carefully place something heavy and flat over each stack, such as a piece of plywood, taking care not to shift the boards, and leave to dry and adhere for several hours, or even overnight.

Trace Your Design

If you're designing your own cat construction, plan ahead and draw a diagram on graph paper before beginning the project. If you're using my Catnip Castle design, take one of the stacked pads, start at one 48-inch edge, and mark the following points with your rule: 6 inches, 21 inches, 27 inches, and 42 inches. Then mark 6 inches up from the bottom at all four points, and rule the lines down to those points. Repeat with the other two stacks.

Saw and Adhere

Saw carefully along the lines drawn. Repeat until all three cardboard stacks have the castle shape. To create the battlements on either side of the central tower, use your rule to draw a line 10 inches down from the top on each, and saw carefully along the lines. Remember to keep your jigsaw moving; if you need to stop in the middle of a line, do not turn off the saw; keep it running or you'll produce a raggedy effect. When you saw through the section that is 15 pads thick, you will need to complete the sawing job with a handsaw (I used a pull saw) or reciprocating saw with a long enough blade.

Check the edges of each section carefully. You want them to be securely glued. If they're not, they will come apart and fan out a bit at the edges. If this happens, carefully use a glue gun to insert hot glue between the boards, and then press them together again.

Glue together the three sections composing the castle, so that you now have a stack of 35 pads. Stacked and glued together, 35 boards will measure approximately 5³/₄ inches deep. As before, weigh them down until they are dry, carefully keeping the edges as flush as possible. Repeat with the three sections that make up the stepping blocks.

Note: If you've cut out the castle and glued the three stacks together, and then you notice a few uneven edges, you can smooth down any offending imperfections with a jigsaw, or a reciprocating saw with a blade at least 6 inches long. Before using the jigsaw to carve out the rectangular steps (15 inches × 30 inches) that lead up to the castle, first make a pilot cut pointing straight down at each corner with your utility/camping knife to ensure the cleanest possible corners.

Size to Fit

Customize the design so that it works most efficiently in your space. The number of corrugated stepping blocks you will need to provide for Kitty to reach the castle depends on the height of your ceiling. If it's low, you'll need only one on each side; higher ceilings will require two on each side. Because the wall at my friend's place where I installed the Catnip Castle is only about 8 feet high, I needed only one step on either side of the castle for Kitty to reach her goal, so I divided one of my 15-inch × 30-inch blocks equally into sections measuring 10 inches × 15 inches each.

If you have a taller ceiling, you can use the 10-inch-long pieces you sawed off to create the battlements as two additional, smaller steps, or saw the third 10-inch × 15-inch section in half. If you'd prefer two taller steps, saw the second 15-inch × 30-inch block in half lengthwise for two 7¹/₂-inch × 30-inch steps, and shorten by sawing as desired.

Alternatively, you can also attach your castle to a wall above a piece of furniture, such as a sofa or chest of drawers. With that configuration, Kitty can use the furniture as a springboard to reach the castle.

Pretty Pet-Friendly

Install

To determine your castle's location, find the studs in your wall. An electronic stud detector is a wonderful thing, and if you know someone who has one, by all means borrow it. If not, you can find one at a large hardware store. I used the more primitive divining method of knocking at the walls (when the sound is low, you're knocking on air; as the pitch gets higher, you're getting closer to a stud).

Note: You'll need different supplies depending on the type of wall. If your wall has aluminum studs (as ours did), you'll need only the supplies listed here, plus a wood bit. If you're working with a brick-and-concrete wall, you'll need to drill holes with a masonry bit, and then use a hammer to insert lag shields measuring $3/8$ inches × $1 3/4$ inches to serve as anchors for the lag bolts.

Use a pencil to mark the wall where the castle's top edge will go, and use a level (this is a large item, and if it's not level, it will look sadly amateurish). It's important that the castle be attached solidly to the wall so that it doesn't wobble; if it moves when Kitty first jumps on it, she won't feel safe jumping on it again. For petite Mademoiselle, I centered two bolts on the central tower plus one for each stepping block. (For a heavier cat or multiple cats, two bolts per stepping block are recommended, plus one centered on each battlement.)

Use a pencil to mark the first drill hole 3 inches up from the bottom of the tower, and the second one 10 inches from the tower top, aligned with the top of the battlements. For the stepping blocks, avoid placing your drill hole at the center, or the block is liable to spin around and deter Kitty. I centered it 3 inches down from the top (narrow) edge.

Using a $3/8$-inch drill bit long enough to go through the 6 inches of cardboard, drill through your pencil markings all the way to the other side.

Have a friend help you hold the castle up to the wall, lining it up with the marks you made for the top edge, and insert a pencil into each hole to mark where you'll be drilling on the wall (this helps ensure accuracy). Then lay the castle back down on the floor and drill 2 inches into the wall at each marked point, with the $^9/_{32}$-inch drill bit.

Put each lag bolt and washer together, and then insert into the drill holes. Using a ratchet, screw each bolt into the wall until snug.

Note: Tighten until the cardboard surrounding the bolts is compressed slightly, as shown (you don't want them to be too tight or too loose).

Say "Here, Kitty Kitty!"

To attract your feline friend to her new playground, rub it thoroughly with organic dried catnip. Crush the catnip between your fingers to release the aroma and make it extra fragrant. Then rub catnip all over the sawed surfaces, using extra for the sides of the central tower to lure her up there. If Kitty isn't compelled to make the initial leap, insert small pieces of her favorite dry treat in the corrugated openings—that'll get her moving.

Mademoiselle the calico cat gets busy connecting with her inner tiger on the wall-mounted Catnip Castle, a simple crafting project you can make that will bring hours of amusement to your kitty—and you, too.

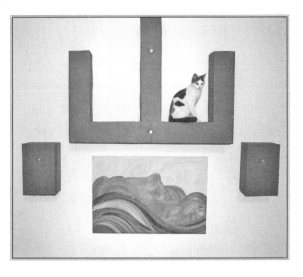

Ready-made Risers

If you don't feel up to the task of custom-building perches for your parlor panthers, a company called KatWALLks will sell you off-the-rack carpeted cat shelves that double as perches and scratchers, ready to be bracketed to the wall in any formation you desire. These perches are inexpensive and available in a range of colors and hardware finishes to coordinate with your existing décor. My favorite is white with silver hardware—the perfect accent for any décor. Cats assume the most intriguing poses on these carpeted platforms. For the more modernist feline, Everyday Studio offers wall-mountable, corrugated cardboard perch-scratchers that look like contemporary abstract sculpture worthy of the famous architect Frank O. Gehry.

Chapter 6 discusses several different ways to "groom your room," by applying the basics of pet grooming to a home's interior. But what if the room could actually groom the pets living in it? That's not such an off-the-wall idea. One clever entrepreneur actually invented a product that grooms animals of all species: the Scratch n All, a colorful system of wall-mounted, interlocking silicone-rubber sheets with bristles that works as a stationary, self-scratching

The smile on Hansel the billy goat's face demonstrates how thoroughly animals of all species enjoy a self-grooming session. In fact, Hansel was so excited upon seeing the Scratch n All pads that he pushed the other goats out of the way even before his owner was done attaching the panels to the wall—he wanted to be first in line to use them! Cats especially love self-grooming—and I've found that providing them with these pads is a great way to offset my guilt at leaving felines alone for hours at a time.

pad. Whenever they feel like it, animals may give themselves a massage by simply rubbing up against a surface where Scratch n All panels have been installed. From horses and donkeys to goats and rescued wildcats, a wide range of creatures enjoy themselves on these vertical self-grooming surfaces. A fringe benefit is that Scratch n All pads can give a quick, inexpensive face-lift to areas of your home or barn that are in need of repair. Brilliant!

Too many cats spend their lives in dreadful boredom, with nothing to do, and a terrible number of them grow fat from a lack of exercise. Whatever form they take, cat shelves and other wall accoutrements help keep our feline population fit, trim, and stimulated. Plus, if there's a dog or two in the equation, and the cat decides she's had enough of the canine's enthusiasm for roughhousing, perches in high places provide an easy "out" for the gravity-defying feline. So I hope more cat owners will apply their creativity to long-neglected walls.

THE ART WORLD GOES TO THE DOGS

Of course, walls have always been showcases for our inner art collector. Each February in New York, two of the city's prestigious auction houses—Doyle New York and Bonhams—host a dog art sale that coincides with the Westminster Kennel Club dog show. That's no accident: Mixed-breed dogs of unknown or unpedigreed parentage rarely got the attention of painters and sculptors, a fact confirmed by the predominance of purebreds in the history of art. (Of course, there's Marcel Duchamp's infamous "ready-made" sculpture, the urinal called *Fountain,* which the Surrealist slyly signed "R. Mutt," but that's conceptual, not representational.)

Now, after centuries of enduring second-class-citizen status, the mighty mutt is finally taking his rightful place in the fine-art firmament. Contemporary animal lovers got an enlightened blast from the past in June 2007, when a portrait of a mongrel named Pointy fetched the whopping hammer price of $432,000 at the world-famed auction house Christie's. This exquisite little painting was the work of none other than John Singer Sargent, the master whose portraits of people hang in prestigious museums all over the world. Today, mutts are showing up in the ateliers of the most talented artists—and so are many other species, from cats and birds to rabbits and aquatic creatures.

Canines on Canvas

I'm the daughter of an artist and a former museum curator, so art appreciation runs in my blood. I've collected numerous works in various media, all depicting animals in some way, shape, or form. As a journalist, I always like to stay on top of trends, and that instinct informs my art collecting as well. And I can tell you that dog art is hot now—which means that it doesn't come cheap. There's even a dealer who specializes only in dog art: Bill Secord of the William Secord Gallery of New York, whose clients include designer Ralph Lauren. And because dog art has become such a coveted commodity, Bill has become a bona fide celebrity!

But collecting animal-themed art doesn't have to be a pastime exclusively for the fabulously wealthy. If you're contemplating starting a collection, here's a tip: Feline art is the next frontier of critter connoisseurship, and since they're less trendy, cat canvases are generally less expensive than depictions of dogs, so it's still possible to find bargains out there. Recently, on eBay, I purchased a nineteenth-century oil painting of kittens at play; when the auction closed, I was the high bidder at $600. A similar painting from the same period representing puppies would have been at least twice the price, so I got a relative bargain. With animal art, it's fun to mix subjects: If you have dogs, collect cat art; if you have cats, collect bird or fish prints, and so forth. That way, your art collection doubles as entertainment for your pets!

Dutch Treat

I happen to love dog-themed sculpture. Three-dimensional artistic representations of beautiful animals can be much more than pretty forms; they can also carry profound symbolic and political meaning. One of my favorite objects is an almost life-size plaster sculpture of a Keeshond by the Dutch artist Claudie Korthals, who was active in France in the 1930s and

This captivating Keeshond sculpture has mesmer-ized me for years. While it awaits a permanent home, the sculpture resides at a New York decora-tive-arts gallery called L'Art de Vivre. More than a pretty figure, the dog is a symbol of liberation—proof that animal-themed art can be as serious as it is beautiful.

1940s. The sculpture is available for sale at Patricia Fuller's lovely Manhattan gallery of decorative arts called L'Art de Vivre, where it has called to me from the window for several years now (unfortunately, at $14,000, the price is still way out of my range).

Patricia obviously has a great eye. The dog is a beauty, reminding me of the lovely Keeshond, named Coosje, whom I rescued, fostered, and adopted out years ago. The Keeshond is a Dutch breed that became known internationally in the late 1700s, when Holland was split into two political factions: the Orangists, who followed William of Orange, and the Patriots. Cornelis de Gyselaar, a Patriot leader, had a nickname ("Kees") and a dog ("hond") who became the emblem of the Dutch Patriot party, thereafter known the world over as Keeshond. Korthals's sculpture was created in the 1940s, during the Nazi occupation of France. By choosing to depict the Keeshond, the artist was clearly sending a subtle message of liberation. My plaster Keeshond is nothing less than a political artwork masquerading as an innocent dog sculpture.

Custom Canine Canvases

While many people enjoy acquiring a vintage or antique painting of someone else's pet, many more prefer to commission living artists to create portraits of their own best friends. With so many artists specializing in pet portraits, in a wide range of styles, today it's easier than ever to enjoy custom portraits of favorite pets in your home. Whatever the medium you choose—painting, photography, silhouette cutting, or sculpture—and whatever your taste, whether classical or contemporary, likenesses of one's beloved animals are a wonderful tribute to the pet depicted.

Many of my favorite dogs and cats happen to be black, but black animals can be quite difficult to capture on film and on canvas. That leaves two options, one incredibly reasonable and the other more expensive (but well worth it). On the affordable end of the budget scale are silhouette cuttings, which depict your pet in profile, usually in black against a white background (but sometimes in other colors, or in white, against a contrasting ground). Simply take a clear photograph of your animal in profile, outdoors in natural light against a contrasting background, and submit it to a silhouette artist for an instant family heirloom.

If you really want to splurge, consider a life-size sculpture of your cat or small dog—or a life-size bust of your large dog. Modeled in clay, then cast in bronze, such a tribute is guaranteed

This silhouette dog portrait was created by Massachusetts artist Carol LeBeaux. This style of portraiture is especially appropriate if your animal happens to be black, as it can be hard to capture dusky animals on film and on canvas.

Sculptor Jennifer Weinik created this life-size bust of my handsome pit bull, Sam. Cast in bronze, it will survive both me and Sam, proudly proclaiming my puppy love for many years to come.

The passing of my cat Ludmilla left a big hole in my heart. This striking portrait, by artist Martha Szabo, captures Ludmilla's spirit essence and has comforted me enormously in her absence.

to outlive you by many years, delighting future generations. It's a lovely way to return the unconditional love that animals so generously bestow on us.

Animal portraits are a great comfort after the animals depicted are gone. The dogs and cats who have left me all are represented by a piece of artwork, or three. Contemplating their ashes or snapshots of them often makes me sad, but gazing at a portrait is always exalting—it's not

a literal depiction, as a photograph is, but a transmogrification. An abstract style of portraiture is especially comforting, precisely because it's not literal. In its web of loose brushstrokes, you can see what you want to see: the animal in his or her youth, or in graceful old age.

Regardless of style or what form they take, the pet portraits I've commissioned help enormously through the grieving process. Thanks to these artworks, my sweet animals exist in another dimension before my eyes. They are truly immortal beloveds.

Danger: Irresistible Dog Collectibles

As any dog-fancying collectibles hound knows, vintage items that depict dogs are a must-have. Now, thanks to one antiques hound's dogged persistence, exquisite examples of a dying art form are alive and well, and available to those of us who are fools for vintage dog paraphernalia.

On her first visit to Kathmandu in Nepal more than twenty years ago, Californian Michelle Page first noticed colorful, one-foot-square metal signboards, hand-painted with images of dogs and the phrase "Beware of Dog." Years later, she noticed the signs started to become an endangered species: They were disappearing in favor of boring, mass-produced plastic signs.

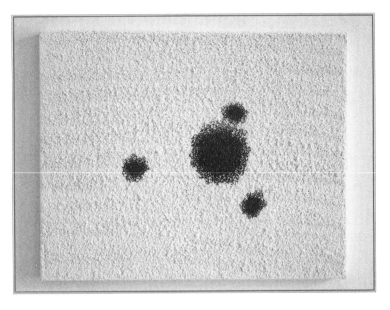

Since the 2005 death of her beloved spotted dog, Tibino, artist Bettina Werner (also known as The Salt Queen) has taken comfort in 101 Dalmatian Paintings, *the gorgeous series of abstract portraits that immortalize Tibino, all created using a special tinted-salt technique that Bettina invented.*

So Page appointed herself the conservator and curator of this folk art form, which she calls "Danger Dogs," scouring shops for fine examples and snapping them up. Today, her business singlehandedly ensures the survival of this art form by commissioning fifty-five different Nepali artists and studios to make the signs, which are then sold at such prestigious places as Los Angeles' Craft and Folk Art Museum shop and the Santa Monica Museum of Art.

"These are original works of art, signed by the artist," says Page, whose slogan is "American dogs, Nepali jobs." She explains, "This really is about the artists." One fan of Danger Dogs is John Walsh, director emeritus of the J. Paul Getty Museum, who bought six. "Michelle has found a whole subculture of self-taught artists living in dodgy circumstances in Kathmandu and brought their delightful work to the West," Walsh says. "All of the signs have fluent Nepalese warnings and delicious, almost-correct English subtitles. There is a lot of sophistication here."

200 mil do domu

DRAMATYCZNE PRZYGODY
DWÓCH PSÓW I KOTA
W BARWNYM FILMIE
**WALTA
DISNEYA**
REŻYSERIA:
FLETCHER MARKLE

Art for Movie Hounds

Animal lovers appreciate a great movie about an animal, especially if the animal looks like one of their pets. Personally, I love movies about dogs, cats, and other pets so much that I even love the movie posters advertising those movies. Movie posters have always been hot collectibles, so collecting pet-movie posters is yet another creative way burgeoning animal-art collectors can enliven their walls.

Did you know that the art of movie posters flourished in, of all places, Poland and Czechoslovakia? Polish and Czech posters designed from the 1940s onward took appreciation of American movies to a whole new level. This makes sense when you consider the historical context: While those countries were under Communist rule, many citizens went to see American movies not just as an escape, but to get to know a country that represented the ideological opposite of the Soviet Union. Because few were permitted to travel in those days, watching movies from the United States was a different sort of trip that provided a glimpse of American culture. The movie posters created by Polish and Czech artists are recognizable not only by their lettering but also by their deeply felt artwork and dynamic graphic design. You can find several online dealers dedicated to collecting fine examples of this art form and offering them for sale to aficionados.

Art A-Fish-Ionado

Photographer Dirk Westphal creates large-format color prints in which different species of fish are captured in various expressive poses as they swim through tanks custom-built by the artist. Westphal's ingenious lighting renders the tank water invisible, so clown anemones, damsel fish, and jewel fish appear to be swimming in pure white space. Studies show that gazing upon the residents of a fish tank is so calming that it can lower a person's blood pressure. But keeping fish can be stressful: If even one thing in their environment goes wrong, they die. For fish appreciators who can't care for these high-maintenance pets, Westphal's photographs are the next best thing to having an aquarium. In fact, the artist says, "They capture features and distinctive markings that the naked eye can't possibly see." What's more, images of gigantic fish are hugely captivating to cats!

3

Style by the Yard

Look around the average home, even one where decorating is not a top priority, and you're bound to find yards and yards of fabric. Just as most of the clothing we wear is made of fabric, so is the majority of the furniture that "dresses" our homes. All sorts of important home furnishings are made of fabric, from bed linens to curtains, tablecloths to slipcovers. Then there are the large upholstered items of furniture (sofa, love seat, chaise, futon, easy chair, or bench) and the smaller, fabric-covered accessories (ottoman, beanbag chair, floor cushion, backrest cushion to facilitate reading in bed, footstool, and decorative throw pillow). And let's not forget fabric window shades!

Added together, that's a lot of fabric—and as anyone who's ever lived with pets knows, most fabrics are easily shredded by curious claws. Materials also become magnets for shedded animal hair and liquid accidents. In chapter 6, I discuss removing shedded hair from a variety of surfaces, but in this chapter, I am more concerned with damage prevention. Yes, you can actually prevent future messes and furniture destruction—and cut down on cleanup time—by selecting stylish, animal-friendly fabrics that are easy to keep clean.

WINDOW OF OPPORTUNITY

In a pet residence, window treatments should be minimal, because heavy, ornate draperies are magnets for pet hair that require a lot of cleaning to stay looking pretty. If you must have curtains, select simple drapery panels that reach the floor (any longer and the fabric will puddle, creating a prime target for not-yet-housetrained puppies to add a puddle of their own). Avoid excessive pleating, elaborate valances, and cumbersome fabric tiebacks—screw an antique glass curtain tieback into the wall instead. These charming decorative items, popular in Victorian times to hold back draperies, come in a variety of colors and shapes, are widely available, and happen to be hugely collectible. They also work beautifully as chic hand towel holders in the kitchen or bathroom.

The only curtains I have are on the window of my first-floor apartment that directly opens on to the street. These draperies are cheap, cheerful, red cotton panels from IKEA that match the numerous red accents I have in that room. The long, red panels have large holes at the top reinforced by chrome grommets, so they're easy to hang from a simple wooden curtain rod—and even easier to remove for washing. I frequently have to throw them in the laundry when they get too hairy from my cats snuggling up to gaze out the window; then, depending on my mood, and which half of *The Odd Couple* I'm channeling, I'll either hang them back on the curtain rod to dry (Oscar) or dry them first and then have them ironed (Felix).

All of my other windows are "dressed" in disposable, pleated-paper shades—the same ones used by house painters as temporary window coverings. These shades are easily cut with scissors to fit any size of window; they stick to the top of the window frame with a self-adhesive strip, and they permit privacy while allowing light to filter gently in. Clipped at the center with a binder clip, they fan out in the most classically elegant "demilune" (half-moon) shape that's very Park Avenue. Surprisingly, I've had passersby remark on these shades with comments like, "They must have cost you a fortune"—that's how good they look. Being made of paper, they resist pet hair, and when they become too dusty or dirty-looking, they're inexpensive enough to just recycle and replace. Brilliant!

Pretty Pet-Friendly

FURNITURE CHOICES: AN ARM AND A LEG

You'll probably be horrified to discover one of the things I've learned as an animal rescuer: Literally thousands of pets are surrendered at animal shelters every year "because they wrecked the furniture." This is one of the most common justifications for dumping a pet. Furniture wreckage can be caused by a variety of animal activities, from vomiting, urination, and defecation to scratching, chewing, and digging. It is true that all of this damage can cost an arm and a leg, in terms of the cost of home furnishings. But I believe it's wrong to consign a pet to an uncertain future—and possibly death—just because the poor animal accidentally harmed a piece of inanimate furniture while doing what came naturally.

Remember, our pets don't deliberately select our fine furnishings as scratching or chewing targets or elimination points out of spite. From a kitten's perspective, it's just second nature to dig one's claws into a nice piece of wood, and from a puppy's point of view, peeing on a fabric surface instinctively feels good because the absorbent material won't splash urine back at them. With time and training, accidents will be much less frequent, even nonexistent, but in the meantime, you can take measures to avoid frustrating cleanup sessions occasioned by pets.

The easy way out is to train pets to stay off the furniture, or to provide them with a castoff item—a faulty fauteuil, odd ottoman, or banged-up bergere—that's all their own to shed on and scratch at. This is a fine compromise, but frankly I prefer to share my home and all its creature comforts with my animals, because it's their habitat, too, and I want them to enjoy it. In fact, watching my pets conked out on the sofa or snoozing in bed makes my day! Besides, having furniture that withstands contact with my pets means I never have to worry about what, ahem, friends and family will do. But enjoying Kodak moments without the stress of cleanup takes a bit of creativity in your decorative choices.

As pet lovers, it's your duty to select home furnishings that will withstand the assault of all your friends and family members: boisterous children and grandkids; tipsy or clumsy houseguests; and yes, pets who scratch, chew, and dig (or occasionally pee in the wrong place at the wrong time). So the arm-and-leg factor needs to be reassessed. Instead of bemoaning what an animal might cost in terms of furniture destruction, be proactive by selecting furniture that won't be so easily destroyed—furniture that can stand up to the normal wear and tear caused by pouncing paws and claws. And the first consideration is the furniture's arms and legs.

If you have a dog who's a champion chewer or a cat with an insatiable urge to scratch, wood-limbed furniture should be avoided. Metal is really the best choice for sofa, chair, table, and bed legs because it's practically indestructible. Another advantage of heavy-metal décor is that it's impervious to damage from termites, bedbugs, and other creepycrawlies that prey on wooden home furnishings. A home outfitted in heavy metal is not only chic, it's extremely sanitary and easy to keep clean.

However, if your style of decorating is strictly traditional and you simply adore wood furnishings, this solution will not appeal to you in the least. In that case, by all means buy upholstered wood furnishings, but please make sure that the wood parts are difficult for pets to reach, and wherever possible, select wood that is light to medium in color, as very dark wood reveals scratches, dings, and bite marks more glaringly. Also, avoid spindly-legged chairs and settees; look instead for sturdy furniture construction. Your sofa should resemble a Bulldog or Mastiff more than a Greyhound.

Here's a great example: A sofa and chairs with fully upholstered arms and back (that is, no wood showing on the arms or back), no fabric skirt at the bottom (a skirtless sofa gathers less dust), legs that are short and tucked under the seat frame so as to confound canine jaws and feline claws—or a headboard that's fully upholstered except for its short, tucked-under legs. A great deal of attractive furniture fits this description and comes in a wide range of price points, and you can customize any of it with your choice of pet-friendly fabric (more on that topic in the "Fabric Selection" section later in this chapter).

If you prefer a mod vintage look to your furnishings, mid-century modern furniture—furniture designed in the 1940s, 1950s, and 1960s—happens to be ideal for pet residences. Hallmarks of this furniture style are clean lines, biomorphic shapes, few hard corners for pets or kids to hurt themselves on, firm upholstery, and either minimal wood for pets to destroy, or a metal frame that's totally impervious to jaws and claws.

Examples of this furniture style can be found in abundance on eBay (by searching the key words "mid-century modern") or at a thrift store near you. Other useful key words would be Heywood-Wakefield, as in the fabulous modern furnishings that are such hot collectibles, or Saarinen, as in Eero Saarinen, the talented architect-designer famed for his elegant upholstered chairs and sofas on sturdy metal bases. Even Saarinen's office furniture was gorgeous, and vintage examples are available at reasonable prices from used-office-furniture dealers.

If you don't have the time for online auctions and aerobic bargain-hunting, here's a simple shortcut: Buy mid-century designs made new today. Heywood-Wakefield makes new furniture with deliberate echoes of its glorious past; Knoll still produces Saarinen's chair and sofa designs, which you can order COM (customer's own material), covered with your choice of pet-friendly fabric. The COM option is also available at Thayer Coggin, which still produces nickel-based upholstered furniture designed by mid-century master Milo Baughman. These sofas and chairs have a timeless air of cool about them, and they're less expensive than the Saarinen designs.

In addition to skirted sofas and chairs, many traditionalists love the luxe, late-Victorian look of tufted upholstery. But attractive though they are, those deep dimples on a sofa, armchair, or chaise are veritable repositories for dust and pet hair—and the puckered fabric that sur-rounds the dimples are a huge challenge to keep clean. Vacuum cleaner attachments are usually too big, so you wind up stuffing sticky tape in there to extract the hairs—only to see new ones appear minutes later. And if the tufting is punctuated by buttons—this style is called (surprise!) button tufting—those buttons might well tempt a bored pup to remove them one by one (and could pose a choking hazard if swallowed). A smooth upholstery style is really the best bet for a pet residence, but if you can't live without some kind of tufting on your couch, opt for a style in which the indentations are not as pronounced, and therefore easier to keep hair- and dust-free (this modernist tufting style is a feature of the iconic Florence Knoll sofa).

FABRIC SELECTION

Choosing the best, most pet-friendly fabric is not difficult if you know what to look for. In fact, browsing textile options is not only fun but also satisfying, if you consider how much cleanup effort you've spared yourself by making the most practical choices.

Wash and Wear

For pet residences, the first rule of fabric selection is washability. When living with pets, every fabric surface in the home should be easy to keep clean, whether the cleaning method used is machine laundering, washing by hand, spot-cleaning, or vacuuming. There's really no place in a pet residence for precious textiles made of silk or brocade, or embellished with exquisite embroidery, or any other fragile textiles that require dry cleaning and kid-glove handling. The fabrics that work best with pets are strong, sturdy machine-washable cotton (canvas or denim) and linen. If you've already spent a mint on furnishings upholstered in something you're afraid to mess up, get denim or linen slipcovers, pronto, for protection. The slipcovers will be your furniture's first line of defense against accidents and will certainly extend their life.

Happily, slipcovering has become a way of life. Most decorative pillows—and floor cushions and dog beds, for that matter—come with zip-off covers for ease of washing, and pet-friendly slipcovers are widely available as off-the-rack options. Many furniture styles also come pre-slipcovered, providing attractive, built-in upholstery protection that zips right off in the event of an accident. These have a nice, tailored look, as opposed to the somewhat more casual, looser fit of the one-shape-fits-all readymades.

If you're a vintage-furniture fiend who can't stand the sight of anything made after 1960, and your vintage or antique furnishings don't fit the mold of readymade slipcovers—and you don't have the time, money, or inclination to reupholster them—consider the option of custom slipcovers. Having slipcovers made costs less than reupholstering, and your friendly neighborhood slipcover fabricator will be happy to make a house call to take measurements, and then create covers that fit your furnishings to a T.

Whether you buy off-the-rack slipcovers or have them custom-tailored, please keep the design simple. Avoid heavily pleated or ornately ruffled skirts, as those fabric folds trap dust and pet hairs. Not only do frilly details instantly up the atmosphere's "girlie" ante (not desirable if guys live there, too), but the fabric dust-traps they create also make cleanup day harder than it has to be. What's more, excessively folded fabric offers ample safe haven to dust mites—definitely not critters you want to risk introducing into your home environment, both for your own sake and that of your pets.

One last point: Do splurge on an extra set of slipcovers. Let's say someone in your home—be they a human with a wineglass or a feline with a hairball—has an accident. The slipcover will absorb the mess, as it was designed to do, but you'll need to strip off the slipcover as soon as possible after the accident, so that the offending substance won't soak through, and you can throw the cover in the wash to erase the evidence. (For tips on what products to use to achieve the cleanest results, see chapter 7.)

While that laundry load is agitating and spinning, you'll need to protect the sofa (or love seat, or easy chair) against the next accident with a clean slipcover. In a pinch, you can always stretch a beach towel or bed sheet over the item of furniture in question to make it less vulnerable to attack while its protective slipcover is temporarily out of commission. If you have

At the home of Kevin and Heather Green, a sandy-hued cotton bed-sheet makes a fine temporary protective barrier for a chaise upholstered in tan Ultrasuede, enabling an unobtrusive tone-on-tone effect. A plus: Bella the Great Dane's coat is a similar shade of tan, so her shedded hairs are less noticeable on this sheet than they would be on any other color.

extra-high aesthetic standards and you'd prefer that your environment not look like it's painting day, even for a few short hours, keep a set of sheets in a pet-friendly shade that coordinates with the color of your upholstery.

Fabric Weaves: How Dense Can You Be?

The density of a fabric's weave will contribute a great deal to the longevity of your upholstered furniture. So, for pet residences, the answer to the above question is, "Not dense enough!" The tighter the weave, the more pet-friendly a fabric will be. You know those times when you apply a lint-roller to your sweater, trying to lift off the pet hair and lint, and you find that many of the hairs have worked their way through the knit to the inside? That's precisely what happens with traditional woven upholstery fabrics such as wool tweed: Pet hairs—especially those of short-coated dogs—poke through the fabric like quills, lodging themselves firmly in the weave, and resisting your most aerobic vacuum-cleaning efforts. And just forget about chenille or boucle; the loopy, nubby texture is fabulous-looking, like a Chanel suit, but it's also hugely intriguing to cats, who view these fabrics as giant scratching surfaces they can't wait to customize by shredding them to bits.

I've seen this happen with my own eyes. One night on the Upper East Side of New York, I salvaged a gorgeous, highly collectible Kroehler armchair, a mid-century treasure that was covered in charcoal gray wool boucle. I couldn't believe anyone would toss out such a treasure, but then that's our modern culture: Everything, from beautiful animals to handsome furniture, is viewed as disposable. I stashed the chair in my cats' habitat until I was ready to send it to my brilliant upholsterer, Lore Decorators, and in that brief time my industrious feline friends saved the Lore team a lot of effort by shredding the fabric, and the stuffing underneath, right down to the wood! It happened again with my Saarinen sofa, which was covered with a wool hopsack-style fabric when I purchased it. Woven wool furnishings are an absolute *don't* when you live with cats.

True Colors (and Patterns)

Living in a pet residence, your choice of fabric type may be somewhat limited, but your choices with regard to fabric color and pattern are not. Know, however, that certain colors and patterns are more forgiving of stains than others.

White is obviously the least forgiving shade for slipcovers, and yet—as I learned completing *Animal House Style*—it's quite popular among animal lovers, precisely because you can see what's there! Of course, keeping white slipcovers looking stylish demands a lot more cleanup effort and results in a great deal of bleach being poured into our already overburdened oceans. If you're going to go the white-slipcover route, please consider using ecologically friendly alternatives to chlorine (for more on that topic, see chapter 7).

Interestingly, black and very dark colors also reveal a lot, especially dog saliva (which, when dry, resembles clear nail polish), so the dark end of the color wheel is to be avoided if you have a giant breed of dog that drools often, such as a Saint Bernard or Great Dane. Then again, one trick of the pet-design trade is to key your upholstery fabrics to your animals' fur. Here's the rationale: In between cleanup sessions, the shedded hairs will be less noticeable on fabric that's the same shade as the hairs!

So, if you have a big, black dog or three, by all means go with basic black upholstery. If you have a blue-gray Weimaraner or Burmese cat, explore that same stunning shade for your upholstery; if you have a chocolate Lab or Gordon Setter, consider rich, chocolatey fabrics. My dog Pepper's coat is a perfect match for a color of Ultrasuede called ginger; when Pepper reclines on a chair upholstered in ginger Ultrasuede, it's tough to tell where the chair ends and the dog begins! (See the "Fabrics That Aren't 'Fabrics' at All" section for more information about Ultrasuede.)

Of course, the happy medium is a light, neutral solid or a print that has, say, a subtle pattern that is extremely forgiving of stains and scuffs. Patterned fabrics in strong colors with white or ivory backgrounds—think chintz, for example—will be more contrasty, so they will reveal a lot more. Toile patterns are gorgeous, but they will reveal as much as the color white. On the other hand, an ivory ground with a subtle umber or gold pattern yields a tone-on-tone effect that hides a multitude of stains.

If you live with dogs and you can't get enough of dog imagery in your home, there are many charming, dog-patterned fabrics to choose from. A few of my favorites are "Unleashed" by Eric Cohler for Lee Jofa, which depicts all the breeds of dog Eric has loved in his life, including his current Standard Poodle Sebastian; "Chiens" by Carleton V, a glamorous red-and-tan toile adorned with hunting hounds; and "Adopt Me" by Tyler Hall (the textile counterpart of the charming wallpaper that appears in chapter 2).

One of my favorite patterns for slipcovers and upholstery happens to be camouflage. Camo cotton comes in a range of colorways, from white-gray-black to army-issue shades of olive green and even yellow-orange-brown. Whatever palette you choose, camo is a dynamic pattern that girls and boys—not to mention women and men!—can usually agree on, and it looks equally at home in a rustic rural cabin as in a sophisticated city setting.

Earth tones such as oatmeal or gray are always winners, whether or not you live with animals: They hide dirt without being oppressively dark, and they look great in traditional and contemporary settings. But it's great fun to experiment with color in your fabric choices, and a brightly hued slipcover or set of throw pillows can be the quickest, easiest way to simultaneously update the look of your pet residence and conceal evidence of the occasional accident.

Fashion pro Kelly Killoren Bensimon styles her New York City apartment with the same panache she applies to her personal wardrobe, and, as befits a fashionista, she recently opted to "think pink" when it came to slipcovering her pair of sofas. Her two young daughters love the Hello Kitty look of the cotton slipcovers, while the adults in Kelly's circle agree that a living room that's coming up roses is the height of chic. As for Kelly's dogs, they don't care what color the sofa is, as long as they have unlimited access to it—and thanks to the slipcovers, they always do.

Fun Furs

Fur is one material that shedded hairs don't stick to, so it's tremendously practical in a pet residence. But I just can't get my head around decorating with dead animal skins for my live animals' comfort—it doesn't seem fair or right to me. So I go with cruelty-free faux fur, which looks just like the real thing and resists shedded pet hairs in style.

Extravagantly Elegant

Fashion designer Isaac Mizrahi believes that no item of furniture should be off-limits to his beloved mutt, Harry. Isaac also adores mohair velvet, and is known to rhapsodize about the remnants he's scored at the Manhattan fabric emporium Harry Zarin. One of the most expensive and elegant upholstery materials, mohair velvet also happens to be extremely tough and durable, having been used for a long time to cover theater seats. That means it has what it takes to stand up to pouncing paws. It does require dry-cleaning, however, so it's not a good idea to have lots of it in a pet residence unless you slipcover your mohair-upholstered pieces with easy-care cotton, linen, or Crypton. But an accent piece covered in mohair is a very justifiable splurge that adds a lot of glamour to a pet residence. Just ask Isaac and Harry!

Techno Textiles

Much as I love natural fibers, the pet-friendliest fabric ever invented—paws down—is a man-made wonder called Crypton. Resistant to stains, moisture, odor, and bacteria, yet with textures that feel as invitingly luxurious as any fragile fabric, Crypton really is a stylish pet lover's best friend, and even comes with its own special cleaning products formulated to melt away truly jaw-dropping stains (including ketchup). Crypton invited several high-profile designers to create patterns, among them the noted dog photographer William Wegman, who naturally responded with several dog-centric patterns, including "Hound in the Round" and "Polka Dog."

On a visit to the penthouse of designer Adrienne Landau, Elsie the red-nose pit bull enjoys a bean bag chair from Adrienne's home collection. It's covered in faux white mink, which feels as plush as it looks and doesn't trap pet hairs.

Pretty Pet-Friendly

In the bedroom of Country Living deputy editor Charlotte Barnard, PeeWee the tabby takes up residence on an armchair covered in off-white Crypton suede.

Crypton got a lot of press, and deservedly so, when it unleashed its dog-friendly Wegman collection, complete with fabric designs featuring silhouettes and scribbles of dogs. These are ideal for vets' offices or children's rooms. But if you're over age 18 and you live with one or more dogs, you might not crave conspicuous canine patterns in your home. I answer to both descriptions, so I naturally gravitate to the solid Crypton colors for my own pet residence, and save the doggy designs for showier, more conversational pieces—such as the Queen Anne–style sofa I made for the 2005 DogHaus decorator show house in Philadelphia, or the pair of Mitchell Gold "chair-and-a-half" seats that dominate the décor of the dog-friendly lounge at Animal Haven Shelter Soho. But if living with dominant dog imagery is not your thing, Crypton also offers an impressive selection of solid-color suedes to suit any style of décor. My favorites are Crypton Suede (an easy-care microfiber) in lipstick (red) and chocolate (brown), grape (purple), and icing (pale periwinkle blue).

Thanks to its proprietary finish, Crypton stays looking new for an impressively long time. It doesn't develop a patina—that lived-in look many people find so appealing about well-worn cotton or linen. Maybe for some people that lack of patina is a deal-breaker, but I find that anything that helps keep my pet residence looking spiffy with minimal effort is a huge plus, so I'm happy to

Style by the Yard

sacrifice patina for good-looking furniture that stays looking good as long as possible. Traditionalists will love the designs Crypton commissioned from architect (and dog lover) Michael Graves, who responded with updates on classic toile inspired by his travels in the Tuscan countryside.

Fabrics That Aren't "Fabrics" at All

Leather has been a popular material for upholstery in pet residences because it's extremely durable and improves in appearance with age and wear. That Ralph Lauren, aristocratic English country look of a well-worn leather sofa is all about patina (the evidence of age), and patina is a *très chic* effect that's easily achieved by furnishing your home with leather and sharing that furniture with pets. The pets will distress the leather with their nails, while simultaneously conditioning it through contact with the oils in their own skin, resulting in the most attractive custom patina imaginable. Leather also stays cool to the touch, which is important to dogs and cats, who seek out cool surfaces because their body temperature is naturally higher than ours.

At the home of Dara Foster of www. pupstyle.com, Flo the Jack Russell gets comfy on a black leather Barcelona couch with black leather straps; this timeless 1930 design by the great architect Ludwig Mies van der Rohe can stand up to pouncing paws.

However, from the perspective of certain dogs, a leather sofa or armchair is one gigantic, fragrant chew toy, the equivalent of a shoe they can gnaw at for days on end. Years ago, just a few days after I arranged to upholster a sofa in dark green leather, one of my dogs chewed the entire thing to shreds in a few short hours; when I returned home, he was hard at work on the last remaining cushion. From this disaster I learned a very valuable lesson: Leather is just too inviting to certain young, orally fixated dogs.

And that's how I discovered Ultrasuede. Ultrasuede is a microfiber—to manufacture it, zillions of microscopic fibers are squished together, rather than woven, creating an impermeable barrier to pet hair. Ultrasuede feels just like real suede and stays cool to the touch, but unlike real leather or suede, it has no delicious leathery aroma to invite violent gnawing. It also resists odors and is easy to spot-clean—both enormous pluses in a pet residence. Plus, it comes in a gorgeous array of colors, from vibrant primary colors to elegantly muted earth tones.

Crystal Clear

I am vehemently opposed to clear vinyl slipcovers as a furniture-protection option. They are tacky in every sense of the term: unattractive; kitschy; and uncomfortably sticky to the touch, for people as well as pets, especially in hot weather. But if, like me, you live with two or more cats, and if one of them suffers from digestive troubles, vinyl can be a clear choice—pun intended!—for creative upholstery because it's blissfully easy to keep clean.

In all honesty, it can get mighty tiresome to clean up kitty hairballs when they're hurled onto fabric slipcovers and upholstered seats. So for my pet residence, I devised a seating option that's fun, functional, and easy on the eyes: Take a vintage chair, paint the frame (or leave it as is), remove the seat, replace the padding with unfurled skeins of thick knitting yarn for a soft, well-cushioned rear-end rest, and then cover the yarn with clear vinyl that attaches to the chair seat with decorative nail heads. All sorts of substances, whether it's my bad (spilled chai latté) or my cats' (feline vomit), wipe clean off with ease. Plus, in winter—and sometimes even in summer, when the air-conditioning feels like an arctic blast—the kitties enjoy sitting on the yarn chairs because they love warm nesting spots, and vinyl conducts body heat efficiently.

As for how the yarn chairs rate from a design perspective, Doris Athineos, an editor at *Traditional Home* magazine—the slogan of which is "Traditional Home, Modern Life"—caught sight of one and featured it in the March 2006 issue. After that, professional interior designer Ghislaine Viñas, whose work has been featured in *O, The Oprah Magazine,* commissioned

Stella the Scottish Fold cat reclines on a white table shaped like a stylized four-leaf clover. The beauty of the table top is preserved by a custom tablecloth made of white vinyl, which stays in place without slipping, and protects the surface beneath from scratches.

Pretty Pet-Friendly

custom yarn chairs for clients—even ones who don't live with pets! When I donated a child-size yarn chair to a charity auction, famed decorator Manuel Noriega-Ortiz was the high bidder, and I later learned that the chair would figure in his redesign of the Mondrian Hotel. And actress-turned-retailer Phoebe Cates Kline does me the honor of selling my one-of-a-kind yarn chairs at her stylish Madison Avenue store, Blue Tree. So in terms of designer cred, clear vinyl can be untouchable if used sparingly—and with a wink.

As with clear vinyl slipcovers, vinyl tablecloths tend to be the height of tackiness. However, solid-color vinyl, like its clear counterpart, can have a useful and high-style application in a pet residence. My friend Lynda Clark has great taste, and she recently purchased a very cool table for her dining area. The table takes the shape of a stylized four-leaf clover, seats eight, and has a brushed-chrome base and white-lacquered top. To protect that pristine white surface from getting dinged by the claws of her two Scottish Fold cats (who, like all felines, enjoy walking and reclining on tables), Lynda took the vinyl tablecloth concept and transformed it into a high-style home accessory. She had her upholsterer stitch up a white vinyl table covering that's the exact same shape and size as the tabletop. The effect is not only practical, but clean and sleek, too—and at Lynda's stylishly protected dining table, there's never any need for coasters, place mats, or a tablecloth! Likewise, if you live with cats and you have a piano, whether an upright, baby grand, or concert grand, it's a good idea to shield the top of the instrument from possible damage by hairballs, so taking a cue from Lynda's table and fabricating a piano cover is a great idea.

BEDS AND BEDDING

You have one bed that you sleep on, but if you're like most pet lovers, you've probably also provided at least two beds for your beloved beasts in addition to granting them access to your own bed. If you're a fashion hound who loves to tweak your décor with the change of seasons, both human and pet beds offer a fun, easy accent statement to help your interior transition from the brights of summer to the darker, earthier tones of fall. And happily, pet product manufacturers are waking up to the need for stylish pet-bed options that aren't cloyingly cute.

Once Upon a Mattress

Pet residences have many strange quirks, and here's a fine example. Box springs—those things on which mattresses rest—are covered underneath by a layer of flimsy, papery fabric. To cats who enjoy spending time under beds (and that's a lot of cats) that fabric layer is simply too inviting to resist scratching to ribbons. This mess is easily prevented by purchasing a couple of inexpensive, cheerful fitted sheets that are the same size as the mattress, and covering the bottom of the box spring with one. When that sheet gathers dust after a while, it's time to toss it in the laundry and switch to the backup sheet. A fringe benefit is that the sides of the box spring will be covered too, and that's much more stylish than leaving them uncovered. You can also coordinate the color of your box spring sheet with the sheets on your mattress for fun mix-or-match effects.

Now that the box spring's bottom is safe, you'll need to protect the topside of the mattress. Remember, there are only so many times you can turn a mattress over once it's been, ahem, breached, and if you've invested money in a quality mattress, such as the pricey organic one I sleep best on, you'll be motivated to extend its life as long as possible. In a pet residence, a mattress pad is a necessity to protect against possible leakage. If you have several large dogs, you might want to practice extra-safe decorating, using not one but two pads for maximum security.

I recommend steering clear of feather pillows and duvets when you live with animals. If they should get punctured by an errant claw, it's no time before you come home to find a snowfall of feathers all over your bedroom. And that cleanup job is a serious drag. Besides, down-filled bedding is a serious chore to wash, requiring tennis balls in the dryer to re-fluff the stuffing. Poly-fill stuffing is best for pet-residence boudoirs, as it's easy to keep clean—and intact.

Between the Sheets

Density of weave is equally important when selecting bed linens as when choosing upholstery fabrics. Those newfangled sheets made of knit T-shirt fabric may be very cozy, but they're totally inappropriate for pet residences, as claws easily catch on them and riddle them with holes. Stick with no-nonsense woven cotton sheets, which come in such a fabulous array of colors and patterns that they can completely transform a room. In terms of price, however, it really pays to avoid cheap sheets and make the investment in better-quality bed linens, and there's a good reason why.

Many pricey styles of sheet proudly proclaim their high thread count, and that high count is very desirable in a pet residence, because the higher the thread count, the tighter the weave. I used to notice that my less-expensive, lower-thread-count sheets would emerge from the dryer with clumps of cat hair still stubbornly stuck to them like so many burrs, while the more expensive, high-thread-count sheets shed those furballs with ease. Painstakingly lint-rolling the sheets is hardly anyone's idea of a good time! You can eliminate that time-consuming step by spending a little extra on nice sheets.

Buying high-quality sheets is especially important if you live with large dogs (40 pounds and over) who are accustomed to sharing your bed. As they leap up to the bed for a snooze, those meaty paws make a serious impact, and loosely woven, lower-thread-count sheets don't stand a chance. You'll hear a roaring rrrr-ip that will, with any luck, be incentive to prevent future damage by spending extra on high-thread-count sheets.

Another way to prevent ripped sheets is to be diligent about covering the bed with a sturdy bedspread that you tuck in along the edges. Think of a bedspread as a protective barrier—essentially, a slipcover for your bed. Matelassé is an attractive style of tight quilting that stands up impressively well to pouncing paws, as all that stitching makes for a tougher, more durable surface. Any color other than white is probably your best bet. On the other hand, you could buy a white bedspread and ask a professional tie-dyer to customize it for you; I did this, with

Making the bed is a grind—unless, that is, you do it with a curious cat who enjoys pouncing and hiding amid billowing sheets. In that case, this most commonly neglected household chore becomes a fun game for procrastinators of all ages.

splendid results. In fact, my tie-dye bedspread's fabulous, free-form, fuchsia pattern is one of my favorite home accents: stunning to look at and quite forgiving of stains.

For an extra layer of bed protection, consider topping off your well-made bed with an industrial-strength moving blanket that you buy at a moving-supply store. These are not the most beautiful textiles out there, but they are certainly functional, and at about $20 each, they're an inexpensive way to protect pricey bed linens. However, even the fiercest tucked bed is no match for digging dogs such as terriers, or for champion burrowers such as Dachshunds. Tenacious dogs won't let a mere bedspread stand in the way of their comfort, and they have all the time in the world, while you're not looking, to customize your bed for their nesting pleasure. So don't think you can skimp on your sheets' quality if you add several "protective" layers on top of them—you'll find out the hard way that shortcuts don't pay in the bedroom.

Incidentally, being diligent about making the bed can be lots of fun with pets in the room. My cats enjoy scampering about among the unfurling sheets, turning this daily chore into fast, free entertainment. Watching them pounce and hide amid billows of high-thread-count cotton sheeting might add a minute or so to the chore, but it's also serious fun. So if your kids beg you to let the family pets sleep in their room, by all means let them. Not only will pets keep the nocturnal monsters away, they could provide just the incentive parents need to encourage children to keep their rooms tidy. Who knows, maybe more kids can be coaxed into making their beds every morning without groaning or fussing!

Pet Beds 101

Everything in this chapter about fabrics can easily be put to the test with a dog bed. Happily, there is a dog bed that's suitable for every room in the home. Dog beds used to be just a matter of style; now they are designed for function, too, with orthopedic features for senior pets and removable, washable fabric covers geared for a variety of different applications around the home. For the high-traffic area off the entrance, there are sturdy dog beds covered in tough nylon. For the living room, there are dog beds that coordinate with fine furniture, providing comfy canine/feline cocooning spots while still looking glamorous.

To the dismay of house-proud hipsters, especially those with modernist tastes, most pet beds are tacky-cute and stuffed with polyurethane foam, which cats just love clawing to shreds. Hepper Home is a collection of cool, classic pet furnishings that are fabulously foam-free.

Outdoor living rooms and kitchens have become the hottest hangouts, and naturally, pets want to share in all the alfresco fun. Indoor-outdoor fabrics are made to withstand whatever the elements can dish out, from torrential rains to blazing ultraviolet rays, so they're great for sharing with boisterous pets. If your dog is too big to feel comfortable on the patio furniture, decorate your deck with a dog bed fashioned from coordinating indoor-outdoor material—and don't worry if you leave it outside in a rainstorm.

Certain fabrics are extremely thermally efficient, especially Polarfleece. This is a "dogsend" for some breeds, such as Chihuahuas or Italian Greyhounds, who have super-short coats and no extra body fat, so they tend to get cold easily. However, certain other breeds, such as Mastiffs, are so hot-blooded that they often overheat indoors even in the dead of winter. For these hot-blooded hounds, avoid Polarfleece in favor of faux suede, which stays cool to the touch. If your hot dog is still panting, try a water-filled dog bed designed to cool down Spot's body temperature.

4

In the Kitchen with Your Galloping Gourrrmets

Here's something pets and their people agree on wholeheartedly and unanimously: The kitchen is one of the most important rooms, if not *the* most important room, in the home. The reason is simple: The kitchen is where food preparation—not to mention snacking—happens. And to our animals, food equals love. If the kitchen is big enough, it's also a place where meals are served, and we all know how much pets love to chow down.

Most important, the kitchen is where pet lovers can prepare meals for pets that not only satisfy hunger but also help promote wellness and longevity while saving money on vet bills. But if the kitchen is a place we'd rather not spend time in because it's not inviting, we'll avoid it as much as possible; so it's a good idea to make the kitchen of a pet residence the hottest room in the house—stylistically speaking.

Cold Comfort

A refrigerator with a door that closes tightly is a necessity in a pet residence. Some dogs happen to be expert at opening refrigerators and approaching the contents as an all-you-can-eat smorgasbord. This is funny—to a point. Take the sad case of Ben, a lovely lab mix with a wonderful personality who wound up surrendered at North Shore Animal League America's shelter not once but three times (!) because of his penchant for opening iceboxes and snacking to his heart's content. If only Ben's first three adopters had added a baby-proofing latch to the fridge, or had a Sub-Zero or Smeg fridge.

These fabulous fridges boast such a dog-proof door that snaps shut so tight, it's even difficult for some humans to open! Besides being substantially functional brands, Sub-Zero and Smeg also happen to be super-stylish. In all, an excellent investment for pet residences where the four-footed foodies are clever enough to overcome any obstacle standing between them and a tasty snack.

Glamorous Smeg refrigerators look like futuristic updates on old-fashioned iceboxes. Plus, the height of the door handle is enough to confound a hungry hound determined to gain access to the frosty treasures within.

More important than the way a kitchen looks is how it feels. My kitchen is where I see my pets at their happiest, and that feeling is infectious. Their eagerness as I prepare their meals never fails to lift my spirits and makes me feel like one of TV's Top Chefs! Once all the food bowls are filled and set before the designated diners, the sound of six dogs happily munching away at their breakfast or supper in harmonic convergence has to be one of the most pleasing ambient noises I can think of.

CHOOSING WHOLESOME, HEALTHY FOOD FOR YOUR PETS

I believe that overcoming my design challenges in the kitchen changed my whole approach to nutrition. Back when the kitchen was U-G-L-Y, I avoided cooking to the point where even making a simple peanut butter sandwich was a major drag. But after I beautified the space a bit and approached it as a canine-feline-design lab, I cozied right up to that stove, stocked and organized the fridge, and became a pretty okay cook. And I confess that my own health has benefited greatly, as has that of my pets.

Which brings me from the fashion of the kitchen to its prime function: feeding and nourishment. It's so true that "you are what you eat," and the keys to wellness, longevity, and disease prevention lie in the kitchen—which also happens to be my animals' favorite hangout.

Today, my kitchen is a pet wellness center. I feed my dogs and cats only premium pet-food brands that I know I can trust. The health and nutrition tips I've learned by feeding my pets to keep them healthy have had a tremendously positive effect on my own health and diet. I've eliminated empty carbohydrates from my pets' diet to prevent them from getting fat, given that obesity can lead to a variety of problems, from ligament rupture to heart disease to diabetes. And since restricting my pets' carb intake, I've disciplined myself to restrict my own as well—and not a moment too soon, because I have a history of heart disease in my family.

The controversy still rages as to whether or not to feed pets "real" (a.k.a. people) food. But food is food, and the rule—for humans as well as pets—is that the less processed and more whole, the better. So by all means share food from your own plate, in moderation, but do keep in mind that certain foods we humans thrive on can be harmful, even toxic to our pets.

Meat is always a good bet to share with pets; as long as you've removed the salt and spices, it won't pose any hazard, and pets adore it. Raw beef bones from the butcher are, from Spot's perspective, the greatest doggie chew toys known to man (just remember to always serve bones raw so they won't splinter and harm a dog's intestinal tract). Fish skins are also full of beneficial omega-3 fatty acids (especially salmon, mackerel, and sardines), as are fish oils.

Broccoli, cauliflower, green beans, carrots, spinach, and peas are wonderful additions to a dog's diet as a snack or kibble seasoning, or as a reducing-diet staple. Dogs tend to love this veggie medley, feeling satisfied after each meal. See the "Battling the Bulge" section later in this chapter for further details.

After puppy- or kittenhood, pets tend to be lactose-intolerant, so please don't give them milk unless it's buttermilk, which is easier to digest. A spoonful of yogurt, on the other hand, is a great addition to a dog's diet, especially if he has recently completed a course of antibiotics (the *lactobacilli* will help restore order to his intestinal flora, which is disturbed by antibiotics). However, some pets don't tolerate yogurt at all—you'll be able to tell by what Spot extrudes eight or so hours after feeding.

For those pets who do tolerate it, a spoonful of yogurt combined with a squirt of flaxseed oil is a great cancer preventive; my pit bull Sam, a cancer warrior, takes yogurt and flaxseed oil with every meal in addition to Neoplasene, the anticancer plant medicine that has kept him in remission for two straight years. If your pet is so sensitive that even yogurt doesn't agree with him, open a powdered acidophilus capsule over his food; these are available at your local health-food store (and while you're at it, take a capsule or two yourself).

Pretty Pet-Friendly

If you feed a mostly dry (kibble) diet, your pet's coat may become dry—and a dry coat will increase the amount of dander and shedded hairs in your home, resulting in more unwanted cleaning activity for you. But this scenario is easily remedied by adding a few drops of flaxseed oil, olive oil, or fish oil to your pet's food, which not only helps moisturize their skin from within, it also sweetens the kibble and—to borrow a phrase from Emeril Lagasse—kicks it up a notch. In the winter, I occasionally add a soft-boiled egg to the mix as well. On those mornings, the bowl gets licked extra-clean.

When feeding birds, use organic produce wherever possible. Wash any and all produce with a nontoxic fruit and vegetable wash to remove traces of petrochemical fertilizers. Even organic produce should be washed before being served to birds, because organic fertilizer (a.k.a. manure), can carry *E. coli* bacteria, and a bird's digestive system can't handle it. Don't buy salad bar ingredients, as they are treated with nitrates to retard spoilage. Birds can eat grapes if they are very well washed; the trouble is this is hard to do. Other produce that's difficult and time-consuming to wash for birds are cauliflower, broccoli, and berries—each floret or berry needs to be washed individually with a vegetable and fruit cleaner, and then thoroughly rinsed.

Take care not to overfeed pets—they will quickly pack on excess pounds, which puts stress on their joints and also puts them at risk for serious health problems such as diabetes. For dogs and cats, don't pull a Rachael Ray and eyeball the amount of kibble; when you love a pet, the bowl always looks half empty because the urge is to shower them with delicious food. Instead, use a measuring cup when distributing dry food, and be strict about it. If your pet is already overweight, slim him down by giving only a fraction of his usual kibble portion mixed in with boiled vegetables until he achieves his fighting weight.

With all the various special dietary needs of my dogs, including the one in remission for cancer (Sam, who can't have sugar, even in the form of sweet potatoes and carrots, because cancer thrives on sugar) and the one with food allergies (that's Pepper, who without

Leaping Lizards

Founder of the Colorado Reptile Humane Society, A.E. Nash collaborated with her husband to customize their Longmont home so it would accommodate a variety of different reptile and amphibian habitats. The house boasts such features as a six-foot turtle tank and garlands of coiled ropes for iguanas to climb on. The resident "igs" are the picture of health, thanks in large part to their diet: hay pellets and raw, shredded leafy greens topped with a homemade puree of dried figs and berries. The name of this green-plate special? "Froot Gloop." It's a real pleasure to observe a troop of apple-green lizards blissfully munching a nutritious meal that's almost as colorful as they are!

At the home base of the Colorado Reptile Humane Society, the resident iguanas enjoy the usual: a home-prepared recipe of fresh fruits, veggies, and salad greens.

substitution can eat only one kind of kibble because it contains just two ingredients, venison and potato), I confess that breakfast and supper preparation in my pet residence takes some doing! But I'm happy to make the extra effort, because I know that the care I take with what I put in my animals' food bowls will help me keep the animals longer.

Toxic Foods and Additives

Some foods that are delicious to us are dangerous—even deadly—for our pets. Onions and garlic are toxic and should be avoided altogether, as should anything containing onion or garlic powder (this includes your favorite chips, so check the ingredients before splitting the bag with Spot). Grapes and raisins are a big no-no for pets, although birds can eat well-washed grapes. Ingesting chocolate is deadly, so anything containing cocoa should be kept high out of reach of inquisitive pets. Apple seeds contain arsenic, so remove them before letting any pet eat an apple core. For birds, avocado and rhubarb are deathly toxic.

Don't give the fatty part of any meat to your pets, and never let them lick your turkey or chicken roasting pan clean—this causes the seriously painful condition known as pancreatitis. Avoid soybeans, chickpeas, lima beans, and any other kind of beans, as they inhibit a pet's absorption of important nutrients. If your dog suffers from arthritis, avoid the nightshade vegetables: green and red peppers, eggplant, potato, and tomato. On the other hand, red pepper, turmeric, cinnamon, cumin, and curry help ease the pain of arthritis, so if your dog can handle a little heat, go ahead; if his stomach gets upset, however, don't give him these spices again.

Chemical additives can also have serious health ramifications. Artificial colors are known carcinogens, and with cancer occurring in 50 percent of dogs and cats over age 10, we need to avoid chemically colored foods. Chemical preservatives trigger episodes in pets with seizure disorder, and if you've ever had an epileptic pet, you know that the goal is to prevent and minimize these painful episodes, not contribute to their frequency.

For years, I fed my cats a canned food that listed menadione as one of its ingredients. I bought this food at a health-food store, and back then (this was before the pet-food recall of 2007), I didn't bother to inquire about all ingredients. Now I know better, and two of the things I've learned are

- Always check the ingredient list, no matter where you purchase the food.
- Menadione, a synthetic "precursor" version of vitamin K, can be harmful to the liver.

My beloved cat Ludmilla, a blue Burmese, died of liver failure at the age of only 10, and I'm convinced feeding her that food contributed to her early demise.

The pet food recall of 2007 was a hard lesson for pet lovers in the importance of reading labels. The first lesson is to avoid wheat gluten, which was the contaminated factor that resulted in thousands of needless animal deaths. Artificial dyes are also known to cause cancer and have no place in your pet's food and treats. Spot doesn't care what color or shape his food takes as long as it tastes good!

The chemical preservative ethoxyquin should be avoided at all costs. Besides causing cancer, it can trigger seizures in pets with epilepsy. But you want your pet's kibble to have some shelf life, so look for foods preserved with tocopherols (that is, vitamin E).

Watching for Allergens

Stomach upset can be caused by food allergies, and that means more cleanup effort for you. But digestive distress can be prevented by paying attention to what your dog or cat eats, reading the ingredient list of pet foods, and eliminating common allergenic ingredients from your pets' diet. Whether you have numerous pets or just one, the goal is to keep them healthy, strong, and away from the vet's office as much as possible. Sick pets are an enormous strain on the heartstrings and the wallet, and they contribute to a chaotic home atmosphere, what with additional chores such as extra outings, special feedings, precise medication schedules, and cleaning up the messy results of digestive upset (diarrhea and/or vomiting). Medicating a critically ill pet can be a full-time job that negatively impacts your housekeeping (antibiotics, for example, have to be administered every twelve hours without fail; certain other medications must be given on an empty stomach . . . aargh!). So I try to do everything I can to prevent animal illness and its

Nothing to Sneeze At

If someone in your home is allergic, please don't automatically abandon the family pet. The person could be allergic to dust from clay or silica cat litter (which is why upgrading to a premium brand is so important; for suggestions, see chapter 6) or toxic ingredients in soap (see chapter 5) and house-cleaning products (chapter 7).

So that the allergic person isn't exposed to the pet while he or she sleeps, make the bedroom a strict no-paw zone, and ask the person to strip off his or her clothes before entering so that allergens aren't carried in. Frequent bathing of the pet in a gentle, emollient, soap-free shampoo (see chapter 5) will also help reduce dander and remove environmental allergens, such as pollen, that may have adhered to the pet's coat while he spent time outdoors. And a good air purifier is a necessity (more on that topic in chapter 8).

---

attendant heartaches and headaches. Food, I've found, is the first line of defense against illness, and feeding a healthy diet can help prevent the need for extra cleanup efforts, too.

Years ago, people didn't believe that pets suffered allergies just as humans do; now, with literally thousands of pets being treated for allergies, we know better. Corn is a common allergen that causes serious stomach upset in dogs and cats, and yet it's a staple of many supermarket pet foods because, until recently, it was dirt cheap. Corn is used to fatten pigs, so if you want to keep your pets slim and trim—and you should—avoid it in their diet. Corn also causes flatulence (in people as well as pets!), which obviously detracts from a home's atmosphere. In general, it's best to opt for a grain-free diet, as grains pack on pounds, which in turn can lead to health problems such as diabetes and heart disease.

Whatever may cause it, tummy upset often requires that pet owners home-cook food for a few days until the trouble blows over. In those instances, veterinarians will prescribe a nice, bland meal of rice or oatmeal and boiled chicken, with the skin removed and the fat skimmed off. This recipe is usually gentle enough on upset canine or feline stomachs to help their digestive systems right themselves. Out in nature—or even in the backyard or the dog park—animals nibble on grass when they feel sick to their stomach—so why not keep a decorative wooden planter filled with organic wheat grass on hand for these moments? Snip off a few leaves and sprinkle them over his food or feed them as a treat. (If you're the juicing type, you can also partake of the green stuff in the form of wheatgrass juice shots.)

Stocking Your Pet Pantry

Let's paws for a moment to discuss a few items that are probably already in yours, and how they can creatively figure in our shared pet project: creating a pretty, pet-friendly pad.

- Plain old white vinegar is a brilliant degreaser, and I know that if my pets lick any areas that were recently swabbed with it, nothing bad will happen to them. This makes it perfect for the kitchen, where everyone's orally fixated mind is on licking, tasting, and eating.

- Walnut oil is not only a fine kibble sweetener, it's delicious with balsamic vinegar on salads, and also conditions wood beautifully, especially any furnishings made of walnut. Years ago, when I had fewer pets and more time, I had a serious antique-collecting habit, and I could always count on walnut oil to help me restore seriously neglected treasures that had grown dry and brittle. Try it and see! Walnut oil is the pet-safest conditioner for wood furnishings. If your pet licks at the wood surface, he or she won't ingest anything harmful.

- A bottle of vodka, kept in the freezer, is a huge help in the event that one of your pets brings home a tick. Splashing a bottle cap full of ice-cold vodka on the tick will stun the varmint long enough for you to carefully remove it from your animal with a precision pair of tweezers. Plus, the alcohol content of the vodka will help disinfect the area.

- Coarse cornmeal is a must-have for cat owners. We've all been there: It's the middle of the night and for whatever reason—it's really humid out, or one of the cats has diarrhea—the cat litter decides to poop out, literally. What to do? The supermarket is open, yes, but don't bring home that icky clay or silica dust that comes with most mass-produced litter brands. The main ingredient of a well-known brand of natural, dust-free cat litter happens to be corn—so one night, finding myself in a pinch, I decided to try substituting coarse cornmeal as a litter pan filler. It worked beautifully. Any supermarket carries this culinary staple, the key ingredient of corn bread—it's absorbent, smells nice, and cats (at least my cats) have no issue with cornmeal as a temporary accommodation. Just make sure you use the coarse variety, as the finer grind will leave you with a big, gluey mess.

TREAT 'EM RIGHT

As vigilant as you need to be about the ingredient panels of pet food, you need to be twice as strict with pet treats. Mass-produced treats are empty carbs that come loaded with all sorts of unhealthy extras—such as salt, sugar, and artificial flavorings and colors—that your pets really don't need. When offering treats, avoid these sinful snacks in favor of high-protein treats, such as jerky-style treats or The Honest Kitchen's cutely named Nuzzles and Smooches. These are meaty and flavorful, and they come in especially handy when training a dog, because let's face it—the best way to motivate a carnivore is with meat. In fact, these treats are so tasty that dogs will often sit without being asked as soon as they see you reach for the package.

Raw bones are nature's own designs, and the nicest gift you can give your pet—large beef ones for dogs, and small chicken bones for cats. Gnawing at them provides hours of fun and helps keep the teeth polished. If you can provide organic raw bones, all the better—just remember to corral pets with raw bones in areas of your home that are easily cleaned (that is, far from upholstered furniture and bedding). *Baked* or fried bones are a choking hazard,

In my house, the crate gets used often to introduce rescued and foster dogs to my permanent pack. For small dogs, there's a high-style confinement option: eiCrate, the first-of-its kind, ovoid, sculptural "cage without corners" by talented designer Peter Pracilio, who's hard at work on a version for big dogs.

however, and can splinter and cause serious injury to a pet's intestinal tract. *Stewed* bones, on the other hand, such as the bones in mom's homemade chicken soup or in Evanger's canned pet food, are soft enough to be safely ingested.

Chew toys made of meat industry by-products—that is, pig's ears, hooves, and rawhide—are a no-no in a pretty pet-friendly pad. Not only are they extremely unsightly, especially when moistened with canine saliva, but they also leave behind a malodorous trail that's a drag to eradicate. They're also a choking hazard, and they often come from questionable meat sources, which are preserved with unsavory nitrates that are bad for pets' health.

Whatever primitive-style treat you choose to give your dog, whether raw or preserved, please separate your pets if you live in a multidog household. Bones and rawhides are so highly prized that they bring out the aggressive beast in the most docile dogs, and they can quickly become bones of contention, resulting in a dogfight. If you live in a small space and haven't got a spare room to separate them, now's an excellent time to bring out the training crate, which offers a

Pretty Pet-Friendly

dog a safe, convenient "room of her own" in which to chew bones to her heart's content. Just please be sure to remove your dog's collar each time before crating her, as the collar could catch on the bars and strangle her. Remember that the classic training crate can come in handy as a useful tool throughout your dog's life. So don't toss it out after your puppy learns not to soil his surroundings; fold it up and store it, as you never know when you may need it again.

BATTLING THE BULGE

Here's a kitchen danger you might not think of: the risk of overfeeding pets, which poses serious hazards to their health. After being put on vet-ordered exercise restriction due to a foot injury, my dog Angus ballooned to 20 pounds heavier than he weighed on the day I met him at the animal shelter. Statistics show that one in every four pets are obese, putting them at risk for diabetes and heart disease (the very same risks carried by overweight people). What's more, because Angus is a large, muscular dog, his excess tonnage also put him at risk for a cruciate ligament rupture.

If you think this can't happen to you, think again. I'm one of the more health-conscious people I know, so empty-calorie, high-carb biscuits are off the menu at my pet residence, where I serve only meaty, high-protein treats. So, how to go about safely trimming down this dog, who was not only named for a cow, but had also grown almost as big as one? The required regimen wouldn't be slim fast, but rather slim slooow.

Veterinarian Jill Elliot immediately suggested scaling back his kibble and making up the difference with generous helpings of vegetables. Angus's veggie portion consisted of frozen organic peas-and-carrots, fresh organic spinach leaves, lettuce, green beans, broccoli, and cauliflower. I'm very lucky that Angus happily eats vegetation, instead of diligently picking out the kibble bits and leaving the green stuff untouched like certain other dogs I know. For between-meal snacks, Angus got bites of romaine and red-leaf lettuce—a treat he still adores, even though he's back to his fighting weight (achieving that goal, incidentally, took about two

Putting the Brakes on Speed Eaters

Large, deep-chested dogs like my pit bulls are at serious risk of gastric torsion (also called bloat) if they eat kibble really fast, follow the meal by drinking gallons of water, and then engage in vigorous exercise. Happily, there's an ingenious product that enables you to put the brakes on speed eaters: the Dog Pause bowl, which is molded in such a way that pets need to eat around a "roadblock" positioned in the center of the dish. This makes dogs eat more slowly, so they savor each bite of every (portion-controlled) meal.

Now, if only a similar solution existed for speed-eating felines. Certain cats I know inhale their food so fast that it comes right back up, which is not only wasteful, but also creates a big mess for me to clean up. One way to slow them down is by pressing canned food around the sides of their bowl, so they have to work hard to lick it off; another is to foster a secure feeling in hungry cats by feeding smaller amounts of food more than twice daily—say, three or four times—so they don't approach every meal as if it's their last.

months). As for me, I trained myself to use a measuring cup instead of "eyeballing" the dog bowls. This simple safety measure goes a long way to keeping pets fit, trim, and gorgeous.

STORAGE SOLUTIONS

Where to keep the pet food? That's a challenge that, for the most part, has been answered by companies manufacturing plastic kibble-storage bins. On the style front, I daresay those plastic storage bins are even more unattractive than the actual food bags they replace! And on the substance side, now that we know more about plastic and its less-than-stellar ability to keep bacteria out, not to mention its tendency to impart trace chemicals to the foods it contains, plastic isn't the safest storage option. Sure, it's "unbreakable" if dropped—but large, determined dogs can easily break into those bins by gnawing them open and devouring the contents.

Pretty Pet-Friendly

It's far preferable to store large bags of opened kibble in a good, old-fashioned, fifty-gallon-capacity, galvanized garbage can that you buy brand-new for that dedicated purpose. These keep critters of all sizes and species, be they pets or pests, from raiding the food supply. Of course, these cans need to be washed out thoroughly with soap and water immediately after purchase, and then dried, because they're treated with oil to prevent rusting in the store. The unopened food bags—my reserves in case an opened bag runs out while the store is closed—I keep stored on my highest kitchen shelf, eight feet off the ground, to deter my canine climbers. This tactic was inspired by one of my dogs, who evidently watched too many episodes of *MacGyver*.

When I've made the mistake of leaving smaller kibble bags laying where the cats could get at them, my feline friends wasted no time applying their teeth and nails to the bag—even those heavy-duty foil models—and helping themselves to heaps and heaps of kibble, which was later extruded in the litter boxes in smelly, hard-to-scoop, liquid clumps. Ugh! So I trained myself to decant kitty kibble, treats, and any pet edible into Ball jars—those glass jars with rubber washers on the lid, closed securely with a metal clamp.

These jars keep bugs out and look wonderfully decorative just sitting there on the shelf, and if I should happen to leave them in the lions' den—I mean, cat suite—I know there's really no way the hungry beasts can pry them open. When I started finding charming vintage specimens of these jars at thrift stores, I slowly began building a collection, and now have amassed several in various sizes and shapes. Instead of an unsightly bag of kibble, I now have attractive jars lined up, Martha Stewart-style. Sweet!

Then, on a visit to the hardware store, I happened to notice that these jars come in head-turningly large sizes, with four-gallon capacity. So I now decant my cat litter and food into those, and the giant jars—resembling the cornmeal and kibble supply of Bigfoot's personal chef—look positively sculptural sitting in the corner on the floor. (This is fine to put in practice with cats and smaller dogs, but not a good solution where large dogs romp; thankfully, the cats haven't tipped these jars over—yet.)

One final word about pet food storage: If you have leftovers from a can of wet cat or dog food, do not—I repeat, do not—slap a plastic lid on the can and stick it in the fridge. Once opened and refrigerated, pet-food cans and their contents wage a cold war, causing what's inside the can to become totally unpalatable to cats and dogs. And if you're a human with a sensitive nose, you too will smell the huge difference between a room-temperature can of cat food and a refrigerated one. The result of improperly refrigerating canned food is a pet who turns up her nose at what you serve her. She's not being finicky; she's absolutely justified in expressing her distaste. For the pet, that means going hungry; and for you, it translates into wasted money and extra cleanup effort.

It's simple to avoid all this hassle by dedicating small plastic food-storage containers exclusively for canned pet food. IKEA sells excellent, inexpensive ones in nesting sets. Just please use tape and a marker to label the containers "pet food," noting (if there's time) the brand and the date you opened the can. These days, canned pet foods come in such tantalizing flavors—duck and quail, to name just two—that unsuspecting fridge raiders might easily wind up re-enacting the priceless episode of *The Honeymooners*, in which Ralph savors dog food on a cracker thinking it is pâté, and then hatches a scheme to sell "delicious mystery appetizer."

Pretty Pet-Friendly

BOWLED OVER

Believe it or not, the dish you use to feed your pet is as important as what goes in the dish. Think fancy pet bowls are a frivolous waste of money? Think again. Plastic bowls are porous, so they harbor bacteria and impart an offputting taste to a finicky pet's food or water. This can lead to drinking and dining abstinence, which ultimately contributes to serious health problems.

The solution is simple: Use nonporous, easy-to-keep-clean bowls, such as the plain, utilitarian stainless-steel ones widely available at pet stores. Some even come with rubber rings to prevent them from tipping over or sliding across the floor. Stainless steel bowls don't have to look utilitarian—many new designs are available that combine metal's functionality with fun, fashionable shapes and decorative resin details.

Feng Shui Feast

Feng shui is the Eastern science of balancing energy (or chi) in one's surroundings for optimal quality of life. Just by sharing our lives, pets help balance this energy, keeping us humans invigorated with their naturally happy, positive energy. To return the favor, there are a few balancing acts we can do for them. Dr. Stacy H. Fuchino, the "East-Meets-West Vet" who practices feng shui for pets at his hospital in California, encourages animal lovers to keep feng shui principles top of mind when it comes to feeding pets.

Dr. Fuchino recommends that you avoid placing their bowls on the kitchen floor. "Food bowls should be elevated off the ground," the vet says. But not too far: "A lot of people feed cats on the kitchen counter, and that's not the greatest thing, because the counter is also a very busy place. There's a lot of commotion in the kitchen as a whole, which is hard on the digestion," adds Dr. Fuchino, who suggests feeding pets in a separate dining area as a solution. Of course, in small spaces that's not an option. In that case, the vet has this advice: "Get an elevated feeder and put it in a peaceful area. This will promote the movement of chi while your pet is eating, and help prevent digestive upset."

If your pets are light on their feet and don't pummel their bowls, ceramic is certainly the prettiest pet-bowl material available, but it's also the most fragile and quickest to crack and break. Ceramic bowls come in a rainbow of colors and styles, so they're easily coordinated with your own tableware. They look lovely just sitting there on the floor.

Another nonporous material that's lightweight and perfect for pet bowls is melamine, which, although not unbreakable, doesn't break nearly as easily as ceramic.

Some bowls are lifted off the floor by feeders, which make the experience of eating and drinking much more comfortable for large, tall dogs. Please don't make your giant dog bend all the way down to the ground to eat or drink; if you think about it, that would mean he's eating in basically the same position he would take if he were vomiting—and if you find that unappetizing, think how unappetizing it is for Spot. When large, tall dogs have to bend this way, the awkward dining position can lead to the potentially fatal condition called gastric torsion (bloat). Instead, serve their meals in a feeder that's raised comfortably off the floor.

HYDRATION HOUNDS

Proper hydration is key to animal wellness, so be sure to make drinking water available at all times, in a clean nonporous bowl. But please don't fill your pet's bowl with tap water; the chlorine and fluoride it contains eat away at tooth enamel and upset the balance of intestinal flora, causing stomach upset. Always used filtered or bottled water, especially if you have birds. Happily, filtration systems are inexpensive and widely available; just make sure you remember to change the filter on time!

Because I have so many pets, filtered water is the way to go, with a filter installed directly on the kitchen faucet. And I love my Aquasana, which uses a selective filtration process combining carbon filtration, ion exchange, and submicron filtration to reduce chlorine, lead, synthetic chemicals, volatile organic compounds (VOCs), sediments, and other nasties, while retaining healthy, natural trace minerals.

Oral disease is a silent dog and cat killer, which makes keeping pets' teeth clean a requirement. Healthy Mouth is a noninvasive oral-care system that reduces bacteria in an animal's mouth by 80 percent, and prevents plaque buildup. Plus, its happy apple-green color is very Martha Stewart, and looks lovely and cheerful in an off-white porcelain water bowl!

Here's a statistic that really bites: 85 percent of dogs and 75 percent of cats get oral disease by age 2. For years, people assumed that "dog breath" was normal—but it's not. A pet with a malodorous mouth is at risk for very serious disease, and even death, as harmful bacteria travel from the gums into the bloodstream. But brushing an animal's teeth is the chore most often neglected by pet owners—especially cat owners, because felines really put up a fight when faced with a toothbrush. I ought to know, because I'm guilty of this neglect myself. My cat Cyrus recently underwent a tooth-cleaning at the vet, and I'm ashamed to say that several of his teeth had to be extracted as a result of my brushing negligence.

Happily, now there's a foolproof system for keeping pets' teeth clean that's as easy as pouring water into a bowl: Healthy Mouth, an enzyme- and chlorophyll-spiked cocktail, with other ingredients like organic blueberry and cinnamon, replaces a pet's regular drinking water. Like Vitamin Water for humans, Healthy Mouth tastes good, is chemical-free, and comes in a pretty color (apple green). Now Cyrus drinks Healthy Mouth every day.

But much more than a drink or decorative addition to your kitchen, Healthy Mouth prevents tooth decay by killing bacteria and softening plaque, preventing buildup above and below the gum line. In vet-conducted clinical trials on rescued greyhounds—who are notorious for having unhealthy mouths—Healthy Mouth was proven to reduce bacteria by 80 percent. That particular statistic always reassures me when one of my dogs presents for a kiss not long after eating poop off the mean streets of New York City.

FIDO-PROOFING YOUR OWN FOOD

I've discussed protecting pantry items from marauding pets, but what about keeping them off your actual plate when you're sitting down to eat a meal? Cats can jump up anywhere, so ain't no table high enough—which means you'll have to train feline friends to respect your dining surface or just close them out of the dining room altogether (if your space permits you this luxury, and you have the heart). Tall dogs can also reach countertop height.

Dogs also prove themselves remarkably nimble when you're not looking, able to leap onto tabletops with a single bound. Some canine breeds, such as Great Danes and mastiffs, have such a height advantage that they can just casually help themselves to whatever's on your plate without so much as stretching a muscle. But even these and other types of tall dogs— who make themselves even taller by standing on their hind legs—can be discouraged from stealing food off your dinner plate with a tall table (of course, this will mean you'll need tall stools as well). The great news is that tall tables come in a wide range of styles that look elegant in any setting. Plus, their height somehow makes one sit up straighter, and makes sitting down to a meal more of a festive, stately occasion—even if it's just a simple salad.

If you like to let your dog wipe your dinner plates clean with their tongues before it's time to do the dishes, and you have one or more large dogs, you'll want to use tableware that can withstand the force of a dog standing on it (which dogs like to do, to ensure they're getting every last delicious lick). In the process of licking your plates clean, dogs don't stand on

Jaidyn the Doberman demonstrates how easy it is for a large dog to gain access to anything delectable you might happen to have sitting on your kitchen counter.

ceremony: They get a firm foothold right on the plate. Make sure the tableware you share with pets is strong enough to roll with the punches. Restaurant-style vitreous china fills the bill nicely, and if it's white or off-white, is a nice, casual alternative even for those of us (me included) who favor bone china, but prefer to protect it from breaking.

Another way to prevent shattered plates and glassware is to avoid using a tablecloth. As animals walk around the dining table, tablecloths frequently get stepped on and dragged to the floor, carrying everything on the table with them. Besides, it's so much more elegant to dine on a bare table—as the enormously appetizing, chocolate-brown-leather-topped ones at New York City's swank South Gate Restaurant prove beyond a doubt. If you find a fabric-free place setting distasteful, by all means compromise by substituting place mats.

SAFETY FIRST—AND LAST AND ALWAYS!

The same commonsense rules of kitchen safety apply to pets as to children—that is, don't leave knives out where they can fall and cause serious injury, and make sure the knobs on the stove can't be accidentally switched on by jumping dogs. But there are (surprise) a few

Even a very tall table won't deter giant dog breeds from swiping anything they think looks good enough to eat, whether or not it's safe for them to ingest—only vigilance and training will. But for smaller breeds, a tall table is a smart choice that outsmarts lawless four-footed foodies.

more safety pointers that are specific to our animal friends, and it's your job to keep them in mind when handling food in and around the kitchen.

- **Garbage** Secure all garbage, especially if it contains fried or baked bones, rocklike fruit pits (a choking hazard), or anything with chocolate in it—this is especially important if your dog is adopted and spent time as a stray in his previous

Pretty Pet-Friendly

life, where every meal might have been his last. Better yet, don't keep garbage around—throw it out promptly, or you might come home to find that Spot has redecorated your kitchen with it.

- **Recycling** Also secure your recycling, as dogs especially love to chomp on empty cat-food tins (as if by doing so they could magically bring back their contents). Those edges are sharp and can cut. Rinse out opened cans of dog and cat food thoroughly so that their scent won't tempt dogs, but also always wear gloves when rinsing out pet-food cans, or you can sustain a serious cut.

- **Grilling** When grilling meat indoors or out, never leave the grill unattended—nothing encourages a dog to swipe food more than sizzling protein, and he could suffer a serious burn while thieving.

Never leave the grill unattended with dogs around, especially tall breeds like Great Danes. Sizzling meat is simply too tempting for dogs to resist, as ravenous Remi reveals, and swiping snacks that hot could result in a serious burn.

- **Hot burners and oven**   Dogs and cats can accidentally turn on stove burners, so make sure the knobs are locked in the off position. If you're cooking something in the oven, such as a roast, take care that a canine or feline culinary critic doesn't stick her head in when you open the oven door, or she could burn herself.

- **Countertop clutter**   Countertops are inviting surfaces for exploration by curious pets, so don't leave anything out that you don't want eaten, chewed, or dashed to the floor and broken.

- **Toxic cleaners**   Household cleaners need to be kept where four-footed explorers won't get into them. This is especially critical if you have a puppy or kitten, who will view anything as a fun toy or foodstuff.

- **Nonstick tools**   If you live with pet birds, evict all kitchen tools—pots, pans, spatulas— that have a nonstick coating, as these produce fumes that are deadly to feathered friends. Also check to make sure your stove doesn't have nonstick features.

- **Antibacterial sponges**   Finally, avoid synthetic sponges that are treated with chemicals to reduce bacteria. You've done all you can to promote your pets' longevity by avoiding chemicals, so don't overlook this hidden danger. Opt for cellulose sponges.

KITCHEN RX: SUPPLEMENTS

Your dog's kibble—if it's a premium brand—comes with the basics that he needs, so add more only as health issues crop up, such as skin sensitivity or frequent digestive trouble. (For specific supplements that help with each situation, consult the Resource Guide at the back of this book.) If your dog suffers stiff joints, consider adding glucosamine to his diet, or a senior-specific supplement. Vigorate, the canine version of the human supplement Juvenon, helps reverse the effects of aging in senior pets. If your pet is quite advanced in years, you can help prevent cardiomyopathy and stave off congestive heart failure by supporting his heart and circulation with the hawthorn plant (which is recommended for humans with heart trouble by no less an authority than renowned cardiac surgeon Dr. Steven Sinatra).

For those times when a light sedative is needed—say, a car trip or recovery from surgery—conventional wisdom has suggested Benadryl, but the herb valerian works just as well, if not better, and it's completely natural, with no side effects. Used medicinally since the Middle Ages, valerian's only drawback it that it tastes extremely awful and needs to be masked with peanut butter, honey, or meat. (Here's a tip: Make a hole in a chunk of grilled chicken, drop the valerian in there, and watch the lot disappear.) Valerian, combined with skullcap, also forms an exciting new therapy for seizure disorder in pets called Lepsilyte, which does not have the side effects of the commonly prescribed drug Phenobarbital.

I've fostered and/or adopted many a rescued dog in my day, and many of them have suffered from virulent strains of kennel cough. Shelter vets automatically prescribe antibiotics, but since kennel cough is viral, the medication rarely helps. What heals this ailment is time, reduced stress, and a healthy diet supplemented with generous helpings of creamy, delicious—and very expensive!—Manuka honey from New Zealand. This stuff is worth what it costs, because it works wonders; I've used it to cure dogs of kennel cough in as little as three days. The antibacterial properties of this honey are such that it's used by hospitals around the world as an effective, soothing treatment for skin infections and burns.

If your pet is taking any kind of medication, from antibiotic to anti-inflammatory, and especially if he's undergoing chemotherapy, you will need to support his liver and kidneys, which over time become ravaged by these medications. The easiest way to do this is with one of nature's most potent antioxidants, milk thistle, which helps to purify the liver and kidneys. This miraculous plant is one major reason I was able to get an extra year and a half of time with my beloved cat Ludmilla after she was diagnosed with liver disease. And for those nights when you've had a little more to drink than you planned—in my case, one too many powerful hibiscus margaritas at New York's Pampano, the restaurant co-owned by tenor Placido Domingo—simply pop two capsules of milk thistle, and by the next morning, you'll be in good shape for the early dog walk.

5

Splish, Splash in the Bath

Any discussion of grooming, whether we're talking animals or humans, ultimately splits into two categories: basics and beauty. For humans as well as pets, the basics would be combing and/or brushing and shampooing; the beauty part is anything additional—the icing on the cake, if you will—such as hair color and cut for a human, styling a Poodle's coat into a show clip, or adding satin ribbons to the hair on a Maltese's head.

Short-haired cats generally keep themselves clean, only occasionally requiring your help; long-haired cats need daily brushing (and some, like my Persian mix Cyrus, often wind up carrying gross excrement on their backsides due to their copious fur, which necessitates bathing and a short clip to keep the area back there clean). But dogs need your help with grooming. And bathing dogs goes a long way toward keeping the interior of your home clean and stylish.

Just as oils and grime build up on our own scalp and hair, the same happens with Spot's coat. The greasy dirt that collects on a dog's hair migrates to the furniture when he sits and reclines on it, and to the walls as he rubs against them. Plus, all sorts of dust, dirt, and mess from the outdoors are magnetically drawn to those oily hairs, and carried into the house on them. All this makes cleanup more difficult, so prevention by bathing is key.

GROOM WITH A VIEW

Many pet owners experience high anxiety while their best friends get professionally groomed, standing around the waiting area and worrying themselves into a frenzy. (I confess I've been guilty of this myself.) That's why grooming professionals agree that the best results are achieved when owners leave pets in the groomer's care and return later to pick them up, because dogs definitely pick up on nervous owners' stress.

"Owners should not stay for grooming," says Tomy Maugeri of New York City's Tomy Maugeri Dog Salon. "Dogs always calm down after the owner leaves. What causes stress," Maugeri adds, "is the owner remaining and the dog believing he is going home. When the owner stays, the dog is torn between his 'parent' and the groomer." At Maugeri's salon, dog lovers have few worries. Besides the convenience of door-to-door shuttle service for pickup and drop-off, they have the option to watch the grooming process online via Webcam.

"We were the first groomer in the country to install a Webcam and streaming video just like daycare centers do," Maugeri explains. For the pets' security and the owners' peace of mind, the Web site is password-protected. Leave it to a Manhattan dog groomer to stay on technology's cutting edge. "Clients can go home, visit our Web site, and keep an eye on their pets," Maugeri concludes. And the sign that says "Smile—You're on Doggy-Cam" ensures that Maugeri's staff is always on their best behavior, too.

WATER WORKS

Your own bathtub makes a logical lavatory, but if it feels at all awkward and uncomfortable, you could be putting your dog and your back at risk, resulting in the need for emergency chiropractic for you both. If your dog is very small, wash her in a sink; if he's a giant breed, wash him in the yard or, if you haven't got one, head for a dog park with a water supply and hose.

The advantages of the latter two options—yard and dog park—are that you can turn bath time into a fun game that your dog won't dread as much as doing time in the tub. In the yard, you can distract Spot by washing him in a dog-bone-shaped plastic kiddie pool that doubles as a fun, refreshing play space on a superhot summer day so that he associates bathing with something positive. If your dog park has plastic pools, great; if not, just making bath time part of your dog's outdoor romp-and-socialize-with-other-dogs-downtime can be enough to help reinforce the idea in Spot's head that bathing equals a good thing.

Heather Green, the talented photographer whose work graces the covers and inside pages of *The American Dog Magazine*, shares her Colorado home with two Great Danes, Bella and Remi, and a Doberman Pinscher named Jaidyn. All three dogs are tall drinks of water and, at five foot ten, so is Heather. So she cleverly designated the bathroom in the basement of her house, where her home office is also located, as the K9 powder room. There's a glass-enclosed shower stall where Heather's husband Kevin showers their dogs while standing up—which is infinitely safer and more comfortable than any bathtub for both him and the dogs.

Wherever you do it, washing a dog takes endurance, patience, and armloads of dry towels that you pre-position so they're ready the second you need them. "Anybody who doesn't know what soap tastes like never washed a dog," said Franklin P. Jones, and he was right. (Whoever he was . . . although many similarly trenchant *bon mots* are attributed to him, Mr. Jones' identity is not clear!) To hurry you along, dogs have a habit of shaking themselves during the bathing process—and that naturally flings suds in your face and, yes, sometimes in your mouth.

Washing a cat is even harder—if you've ever had to do this chore, you know how much cats loathe getting wet, struggling and putting up an admirable fight the entire time, hooking their claws into any available surface, including your legs. Of course, you can always make an appointment with a groomer, but this is, (a) costly, and (b) not always trustworthy, as horrific news accounts of small pets sustaining injury or getting fried to death by rogue hair dryers

attest. If you're going to engage the services of a professional groomer, please take the time to ask your vet and other pet owners for recommendations, so you're sure to find someone you and your pet can trust. And please be sure the groomer uses a nontoxic brand of shampoo (you'll see why in the "In a Lather: Checking the Ingredients of Pet Shampoos" section).

In New York City, where I live with my pets, there's a great place called Beverly Hill's LaunderMutt, and as its name suggests, it's a Laundromat where you can go to wash your dog, just as you go out to wash your clothes. Happily, more and more such self-service businesses are opening around the country—like the excellent Sudsy Dog in Lakewood, California—that allow pet owners to bathe their own pets in the comfort of a setup entirely geared to facilitating this activity. Establishments like Sudsy Dog offer waist-high tubs expressly designed to simplify the difficult chore of bathing pets, clips to attach your dog's collar/leash to the wall, plus a full menu of all-natural grooming products. Best of all, they take care of the cleanup afterward, including washing and drying the soggy towels. Being

Pretty Pet-Friendly

Alfresco Bathing

New products have been invented to make washing dogs in your backyard as easy as possible for you and your pet, including portable pet tubs that assemble quickly and fold up for ease of storage. One model even comes with a no-slip cushioned mat, a three-point adjustable harness to politely immobilize uncooperative canine customers, and a booster ramp to give senior dogs a leg up going in and coming out. Brilliant!

For small, sensitive dogs who don't appreciate the military-style, cold-shower treatment of the garden hose, there are also simple devices that connect to your washing-machine hose to mix warm and cold water to a comfortably lukewarm temperature, with a handle that offers variable spray strengths.

spared the tough haul of tons of terry cloth to the Laundromat (or doing several loads in your own washer/dryer) is a huge service that's easily worth twice the price of admission!

It goes without saying that if you're designing your own home from scratch with an architect, you can create a dream laundry room that houses not only a superefficient washer-dryer for your family's clothing and other washables but also a waist-high sink for washing the family pet. In this dream laundry room, it's no problem to use as many towels as you need to dry off the family dog after a bath—just toss them in the nearby oversized washing machine immediately after you're done!

RUB-A-DUB-TUB

If you're going to undertake a pet primping project in your own bathtub, make sure the tub is clean and free of soap scum so Spot won't hurt himself (or you) by sliding around. Then take the precaution of laying down a rubber nonskid mat on the tub floor, to give somewhat secure footing during the bathing process.

Start by Deshedding

Bathing a dog will cause a lot of hairs to shed, so before you even think about giving Spot a wet bath, "dry clean" him with a good brushing (a de-shedding tool makes this chore fast and easy; more on that topic in chapter 6). If you don't, your bathtub will look like an homage to *Le Déjeuner en Fourrure,* a.k.a. the "Fur Teacup," Meret Oppenheim's famous surrealist sculpture at the Museum of Modern Art. And that means more cleanup effort for you later, so it's definitely to be avoided.

Even after a thorough de-shedding session, however, you'll need to protect your plumbing from becoming overloaded with gobs of shedded pet hair, which will promptly attach themselves to the tub, walls, floors, and pipes. Where you definitely don't want the hairs to wind up is down the drain. A professional plumber can always snake the drain clean with a power tool, but this service is costly, so prevent (or at least postpone) the need for it by buying an inexpensive plastic drain trap at the hardware store, and continuously clearing it of shedded pet hairs while you wash Spot.

Please protect Spot's ears by plugging them with rolled cotton before you begin the wet-down phase of the bath. Pets, like humans, can get swimmer's ear if water makes its way into the ear canal. Take this simple precaution, and you get a reward: After you're done bathing your pet, you can remove the cotton along with any brown gunk that comes with it (ear goo is softened and primed for removal by the wet conditions of the task at hand), thereby simplifying the ear-cleaning process.

Every once in a while, a dog or cat will express fluid from their anal sacs that smells godawful— and to make matters even more malodorous, the poor pet might scoot his butt along on any surface that helps relieve that uncomfortable feeling back there, thereby transferring the horrid odor to your furnishings. When shampooing, pay extra attention to your pet's rear end and the undertail area after such an episode to be sure you haven't left anything behind that could come off on your furnishings. And be especially gentle with rinsing back there—never aim a hose or shower head directly at the undertail area at full force. Always approach with your water source gently, with a light spray, from each side, until you've carefully showered off the suds and, with them, the stench.

Finally, remember that the body temperature of dogs and cats is naturally higher than ours, so don't allow too much steam to build up in the bathroom as you're bathing Spot. Feeling overheated will only make her more uncomfortable and possibly uncooperative. Leave the bathroom window open for some much-needed air and only use lukewarm water to wet down pets.

Lather, Rinse, Repeat

You can work up a lather the old-fashioned way—with your fingers—or you can make bath time a spa escape for Spot by using a specially designed rubber brush with a shampoo reservoir to dispense the sudsy stuff and soft rubber bristles to provide tingling K9 massage action. Rub him the right way, and who knows, maybe your dog might even look forward to his next bath! Even if you do use one of these handy brushes, take a moment to let your hands travel carefully along your dog's sudsy body. Besides turning bath time into bonding time, this extra step has enormous value as a preventive healthcare measure.

Bath-time stroking is the equivalent of the breast cancer self-exam for women, because what you're doing is feeling for lumps that may have sprouted under your dog's skin, unbeknown to you and possibly camouflaged by his coat, especially if it's thick and fuzzy. If you do find a lump, have it examined by a vet without delay—this is how I learned that my dog Sam had cancerous mast-cell tumors. Mercifully, I was able to catch them in time to treat them, and today, eight years later, fourteen-year-old Sam is still going strong!

When washing your dog's face, use the same commonsense guidelines you use when applying shampoo to your own head or that of your child: Avoid the eyes. If your pet has long hair, consider finishing up bath time with an emollient conditioner; dry haircoats gnarl up more easily, and moisturizing the haircoat helps to prevent tangling and matting.

To make sure you rinse shampoo thoroughly out of Spot's coat from head to tail, you'll need a good hand-shower attachment. If you're washing Spot outdoors, the average garden hose offers a powerful jet, which, though less precise than a hand-shower attachment, is just the thing to rinse soap clear out of a thick-pelted large dog's coat. But such a jet is way too strong—and too cold—for small, fragile pets. Use common sense and don't subject pets to water torture: The less pleasant the experience, the more small pets will—understandably!—become hugely fearful of the bathing process. So for your own sake as well as theirs, please go easy on them.

Drying Off

Ordinary terry cloth, even if it's the thickest, plushest Turkish-style towel, is no match for a long-haired pet's thoroughly saturated haircoat. All cats, and many dogs, dislike being wet and will shake themselves off vigorously in an attempt to rid themselves of that sinking soaking feeling. You can help pets feel more comfortable after a bath—and make the drying-off process faster and more efficient—by using a high-tech towel for the postbath rubdown. These are specifically designed for drying pets off after a bath (or a dip in the pool or pond), and even come with corner pockets—picture a towel ending in two or four oven mitts, and you get the idea—to make the drying-off process easier still. In cold weather, an efficient, fast-drying towel also helps prevent Spot from catching a chill.

No matter how thoroughly you towel-dry Spot, he will still rub his soaked body against any available surface, turning your sofa, your bed, his dog bed, and miscellaneous other furnishings into giant sponges as he tries to shed every last drop of moisture on his coat. To avoid putting a damper on your entire home environment, contain just-washed pets as much as possible immediately after they're bathed, placing old, dry, terry-cloth towels on the floor for them to roll around on. If you can't contain them, use the old, dry towels to cover the most vulnerable surfaces. And if you chauffeur Spot to a self-service dog-wash, remember to bring towels and/or an old sheet to protect your vehicle's backseat for the drive home.

IN A LATHER: CHECKING THE INGREDIENTS OF PET SHAMPOOS

What you wash your pet with is as important as where and how you wash her. The frightening pet-food recall of 2007 taught pet owners the importance of reading ingredient panels on food packages to avoid potentially harmful gluten, preservatives, and artificial preservatives and colors. But food isn't the only pet product animal lovers need to be careful about.

Most mass-produced shampoos contain ingredients that are unnecessarily harsh on pets' skin. These include sodium lauryl sulfate (SLS) or sodium laureth sulfate (harsh degreasers and foaming agents, a.k.a. "surfactants," known to cause skin irritation in clinical tests like the infamous Draize test); chemical preservatives such as DMDM hydantoin (it releases formaldehyde, a suspected cancer-causing toxin); and anything ending with the chemical suffix -paraben (such as methylparaben or propylparaben).

Propylene glycol, which is used as a humectant in grooming products, is the same as antifreeze (which is highly toxic to pets whether ingested orally or absorbed via the skin). The substance irritates skin while causing liver abnormalities and kidney damage. Additional shampoo ingredients to avoid are phthalates, such as diethyl phthalate (DEP). These are hormone-disrupting chemicals suspected of contaminating breast milk and causing damage to the kidneys, liver, lungs, and reproductive organs. A study found that DEP is damaging to the DNA of sperm in adult men. If you use pet shampoos containing these toxic ingredients, you expose not only your best friend to them but yourself as well.

Research has shown that SLS, for example, may cause potentially carcinogenic nitrates and dioxins to form in the shampoo bottle by reacting with other ingredients—and large amounts of nitrates may enter the bloodstream via the skin from just one shampooing (they are also retained in the tissues for up to five days). In its report on the safety of SLS, the *International Journal of Toxicology* notes that this ingredient has a "degenerative effect on the cell membranes because of its protein denaturing properties" and that "high levels of skin penetration may occur at even low use concentration."

Incidentally, the toxic ingredients listed in the preceding paragraphs are also widely used in beauty products for humans, so it's my hope that reading the ingredient panel on your pet's personal-care products will inspire you to do the same with your own and those you use on your kids. Pets have a limited life span, and many of mine have already bravely battled life-threatening diseases, including cancer. I don't wish to risk their health or compromise their longevity by adding toxic, potentially carcinogenic shampoo to their routine, exposing them to it when they're at their most vulnerable, with their hair and skin wet and their pores wide open.

Before I learned about SLS, I was a big fan of a certain shampoo made for pets and people to share. Of course it contained SLS, and we used it at home all the time because we just didn't know better. Before throwing this stuff out, I was curious to see how it would clean a really tough mess: the sidewalk that adjoins my apartment building's stoop, where the concrete had become pitifully streaked with urine (though not by my dogs!). So I squeezed out a few drops of shampoo and rinsed the area off with a few gallons of water. After drying in the sun, the urine streaks vanished. Talk about industrial strength! This product's ability to clean concrete made sense after I learned of the industrial uses of SLS, which include garage floor cleaners, engine degreasers, and car wash soaps. So I kept my remaining supply around for the purpose of polishing the sidewalk, and never used the product again.

You definitely don't want to use shampoo containing SLS on a regular basis, but there might be a few instances when it comes in handy. Let's say you live in the city, and your dog peers under a parked car to look for chicken bones, emerging with a big black streak of grease across his shoulders or forehead—or he walks through a patch of asphalt that's slick with motor oil. Or he gets hit with pigeon poop from above. Or let's say you've spent a day at the beach and the dog went for a swim—the sea, sadly, is so full of slimy pollution that immersion in it is bound to leave a greasy residue on Spot's skin. Ponds and lakes aren't as clean as they were decades ago, so after a dip, Spot will definitely be due for a bath. For these instances, I recommend Fur, a product that strangely combines SLS with the lovely botanical ingredient Moringa seed extract, which is highly emollient and contains antiseptic and anti-inflammatory properties that help heal insect bites, rashes, and burns. (Or, in a pinch, just use baby shampoo, of which—shockingly—SLS is a main ingredient, despite findings that it can cause harm to children's developing eyes.) Please counteract the potentially harmful effects of SLS by sprinkling milk thistle over your dog's food for a couple of days after his bath, to protect his liver and kidneys (for more on that topic, see chapter 4).

In a much more dramatic turn of events, dogs have been known to wind up in New York's East and Hudson Rivers, accidentally or intentionally. The lucky ones—like a mutt named Gracie belonging to a filmmaker friend of *Sopranos* star Edie Falco, who jumped a fence while out walking with the actress, plunging into the Hudson River and treading water for twenty minutes before she was rescued by emergency service officers—have been pulled from danger. But the horrific soup of sludge that New York's rivers have become through years of pollution necessitates washing off any creature who takes a dip in it with an industrial-strength surfactant—and for that SLS does the job. Again, another job for Fur or baby shampoo—and another occasion to supplement your dog's diet with milk thistle.

While some pets don't experience adverse reactions to products containing SLS, sensitive or allergic animals become miserably itchy—and when they scratch, their skin becomes infected, requiring a visit to a veterinary dermatology specialist. This is a serious problem for white-coated urban dogs who are magnets for urban grime and, therefore, get groomed more frequently.

Botanical Bath

Happily, there are several pet shampoos that contain only natural, nontoxic ingredients. Organimals shampoo by Aubrey Organics replaces chemical preservatives with citrus-seed extract and vitamins A, C, and E. Preserved with rosemary extract, Vermont Soap Organics pet shampoo contains coconut and jojoba oils, plus aloe vera, and is the first USDA-certified organic pet shampoo.

My pit bulls have extremely sensitive skin, and one of them suffers from allergies, so I wash all my dogs in TheraNeem Pet Shampoo by OrganixSouth, which is soap-free and contains skin-soothing arnica. The formula is very emollient, so it won't dry out a dog's dermis, and it's especially good for pets suffering from mild dermatitis or psoriasis. A question that's frequently asked by dog lovers is: How often can I safely wash my sensitive-skinned pet? With a gentle, soap-free formula like TheraNeem Pet Shampoo, the answer is as often as the spirit moves you—especially if your dog suffers from environmental allergies. Go ahead and wash all that pollen and other irritating matter off every other day, or even daily, before it has a chance to cause a bad reaction.

Pathogenic Pesticides

Fleas and mosquitoes are a disease-carrying scourge, to be sure; fleas transmit anemia and tapeworm, and mosquitoes carry heartworm. But chemical preventives work by introducing insecticide into your pet's bloodstream—in order to die, the pest has to take a bite out of your best friend, and the bite often causes an allergic reaction that leads to itching and infection. What's more, it's not great for people, especially kids, to touch the part of the animal's coat that has been treated with the chemical—you're introducing a toxic chemical into your home atmosphere, which is especially harmful if you have kids, who touch everything, then stick their hands in their mouths. Instead, use a botanical alternative, as discussed in the "Pest-Prevention Alternatives" section of this chapter.

Another soap-free shampoo is the pleasantly berry-scented Tropiclean, which is sold at Petco and claims not to interfere with Frontline and other topical pest preventives. Which brings us to another important discussion: natural pest prevention. See the "Pathogenic Pesticides" sidebar for details.

Pest-Prevention Alternatives

Fortunately, there are botanical alternatives to vet-prescribed pest-preventive medications. One is neem oil, an extract of the mahogany tree that's wonderfully emollient and proven to heal skin irritations, in humans and animals, ranging from psoriasis to chemical burns. But neem oil's most wonderful feature is its natural insecticide property; it smells like the most pungent garlic you've ever encountered, and once absorbed into the bloodstream through the skin via TheraNeem shampoo, neem actually makes the blood taste bad to pests, so they won't bite your best friend. And you've neatly avoided the allergic reaction that many pets experience from fleabites. (Happily, shampoos containing neem mask the garlicky odor successfully with other, much nicer-smelling ingredients!)

For monstrously mosquito-infested areas, buy a separate bottle of straight neem oil, and add a few drops of it to TheraNeem shampoo—or Tropiclean, or any nontoxic shampoo you like—in your palm immediately before you lather up your pet. It's a thick, viscous oil, so this works better than direct application as a way to carry it across your animal's skin.

Ticks, which are not insects but arachnids, are much harder to repel, and they carry such horrors as babesiosis, ehrlichiosis, Lyme disease, and tick paralysis—so a little neem alone won't do the trick. Thankfully, Buck Mountain Botanicals in Montana has developed the ultimate tick repellent: Parasite Dust, a totally safe, nontoxic combination of neem, diatom flour, and yarrow in powder form. This product is a dogsend: A level teaspoon, worked through the fur and into the skin of your dog or cat (or horse), will protect him from ticks (plus flies, mosquitoes, and fleas, too). If you can see it on your pet's coat, you've used too much. When your

pet gets wet, it's time to reapply (but normal self-grooming by cats won't necessitate reapplication). For maximum protection in the summertime, I use both neem oil–boosted TheraNeem Pet shampoo and Parasite Dust on my pets. And if there's any concern that a dog may have brought fleas into the house, simply sprinkle Parasite Dust liberally over the suspicious areas, wait a few minutes, and then vacuum. (See more detailed advice for handling this situation in chapter 9.)

SPOT-CLEANING SPOT

For in-between times that require a quick spot-clean but not an entire bathing production, there are many grooming products available that help prevent pets from bringing the outdoors in and paw-printing your décor. These range from soft, synthetic-microfiber gloves that help you wipe pets' paws, soaking up mud and moisture before it can tattoo itself all over your home, to dispensers containing paw-wipes saturated with safe, soothing botanical extracts that both clean and moisturize a dog's paw pads. Neatniks especially appreciate these handy helpers when the weather forecast calls for rain and/or snow, both conditions that mean dogs will come home with muddy paws or worse (such as snow-melting salt; for more on that topic, see chapter 9). A quick wipe will prevent pets from tattooing your décor with paw prints.

On snowy days when the streets are paved with harsh ice-melting salt, I used to position bowls of warm water by the door so that I could dunk my dogs' salty paws into them, then wipe them dry. Needless to say, the cleanup led to lot of spillage and even more cleanup. Other dog lovers who find themselves frustrated by this situation can now use a product called the Paw Plunger (see chapter 6). This clever device contains water neatly while you dip Spot's extremities inside for a quick footbath. It's important to dry the paw pads thoroughly, so use a highly absorbent microfiber glove to get in between the toes.

SKUNK ATTACK

When anal-sac expression happens to a dog or cat, it's involuntary, but there is one animal who can control when, where, and on whom he expresses: the skunk. No odor, no matter how pungent, rivals what comes out of a none-too-happy skunk. If your only experience of skunks is the animated antics of the *Looney Tunes*' Pepé Le Pew or adorable Flower of *Bambi* fame, consider yourself very lucky. These black-and-white backyard critters are armed with a defense mechanism like no other: anal scent glands that spray powerfully foul-smelling sulfurous chemicals. The unbelievably gross smell of skunk easily qualifies as the worst odor on Earth, with distinctive top notes of rotten eggs, garlic, and burnt rubber. Mmm! So offensive is this smell that it can repel bears; so irritating, it can make the afflicted want to climb out of their very skin (and if it hits the eye, it can cause temporary blindness).

Natural selection has made skunks expert at chemical warfare, capable of accurately hitting any potentially threatening target—be it canine, feline, human, or ursine—from as far away as 10 feet.

Think stink: Your unsuspecting country dog, enjoying the refreshing night air as he snuffles about on his late-evening, pre-bedtime outing, might suddenly get the shock of his little life if he crosses paths with one of these ticking stink bombs. He'll immediately seek the safe haven of home—then proceed to rub his poor, malodorous self all over every surface of your interior in a desperate, frantic attempt to escape the torturous stench that envelops him.

A Skunk Home Remedy

Even if you think this scenario can't happen to you, be prepared to deal with it when it does. Just forget the persistent myth about tomato juice: It does not work. (Some of us learned this the hard way only after dumping gallons of the thick, red stuff on our pitiful pups, to no avail.) The only home remedy that effectively removes skunk odor is a homemade potion so powerful, it cannot be bottled or it will combust: a mix of hydrogen peroxide, baking soda, and liquid detergent that must be prepared fresh before each use. Contain your dog in an area that's nonporous and easy to clean, such as the tiled surfaces of the kitchen or bathroom, and mix up the tried-and-true formula for neutralizing skunk spray. Here's the homemade formula for de-skunking:

- 1 quart of 3% hydrogen peroxide
- 1/4 cup baking soda
- 1 teaspoon Dawn liquid soap

In a ceramic, metal, or glass bowl (not wood or plastic), combine the ingredients, which will foam up like a particularly impressive science project or wizard's potion. Take care to wear rubber gloves when handling your dog, or the scent of skunk will stay on your hands for days (and you may forget, as I did, and then rub your eyes . . . ouch). Bathe your dog in the just-mixed solution, taking care to avoid Spot's eyes—it's very caustic—and then rinse him thoroughly in water. If your dog got it in the eyes, see if he'll let you gently flush his peepers with sterile saline solution (the same kind used to clean contact lenses), to reduce the irritation caused by the skunk spray.

As a rule, I recommend using only chemical-free "green" cleaners, but in the special case of a skunking, you really need to make an exception and use Dawn liquid in this recipe. The reason is that the powerful chemical degreaser it contains (lauryl sulfate, discussed in the "In a Lather: Checking the Ingredients of Pet Shampoos" section earlier in this chapter) will help erase any trace of oily skunk spray. So always keep a small bottle of Dawn handy in your home, because in this application it's a lifesaver—as it was when wildlife rescuers used it to bathe the birds, otters, and other unfortunate creatures who got oil-slicked after *Exxon Valdez* tanked.

Hemp Power

A recent invention that's an absolute dogsend is Omega Zapp Conditioning Skunk Odor Pet Shampoo by NuHemp Botanicals. This gentle, all-natural stuff contains no SLS or other harsh chemicals and smells very pleasant—its active ingredient is organic hemp oil—yet it manages to thoroughly neutralize *eau de mouffette* (as Pepé Le Pew would describe skunk funk *en français*). Omega Zapp is especially helpful if your dog has been skunked full in the face, around the eyes, where you must not apply the foaming peroxide-baking soda brew described in the preceding section.

Charles Darwin—yes, that Charles Darwin—wrote ominously of skunk spray, "Whatever is once polluted by it is for ever useless" (we trust he didn't mean skunked pets), but thankfully, technology now makes it possible to keep furnishings and clothing that have come in contact with this singular stench. Omega Zapp works great on laundry—I use it to extend the life of stinky T-shirts by pretreating the armpits with it. In fact, I confess I've become something of an Omega Zapp addict, even using it as a shower gel on myself after working up a particularly nasty sweat (it's great for smelly feet), and occasionally using it on the dogs even if they haven't been skunked. Blame it on the hemp oil!

City dogs don't generally tangle with skunks, but there's another troublesome mess Spot might bring home after a walk through the concrete jungle: molten chewing gum, which morphs into a horrifically gooey, seemingly indelible slime after just a few seconds' griddling in the midday sun.

To remove chewing gum from a dog's paw pad, rub it with something nice and oily that you have on hand: organic peanut butter, margarine, Crisco, mayonnaise, or olive oil. But since many of these things are quite palatable to Spot, I've found it difficult to keep dogs from wanting to eat the stuff off their foot as I'm struggling to remove the gum, and gum contains Xylitol, which is toxic to pets, so I prefer orange oil (which tastes bad to pets and has other useful applications in a pet residence, as you'll learn in chapter 9) or neem oil, which just plain tastes bad.

Equally sticky, in their own way, are burrs, which I am convinced must have inspired the inventors of Velcro to create their moneymaker. One short romp in the woods and your long-haired dog will return with sticky burrs lodged in his thick fur. Recently, my Chow-Rottweiler mix Tiki came back with a particularly bad case of burrs; his normally majestic plume tail was completely covered in them, down to the skin. I wound up spending hours using my fingers to slowly, gently remove these nasties from my poor dog's coat and tail before serious matting had a chance to set in.

Master weaver Paula Chaffee Scardamalia offers excellent advice for removing burrs, gleaned from years of experience detangling not only the yarns she works with but the coat of her beloved Collie, Duncan, who "will stand or sit with dog-saintly forbearance while we remove burrs, because we have learned the secret." Here's the secret: "To not pull the burr away from the dog, but to pull the dog hair away from the burr. By holding onto the burr and gently pulling the hair away from the burr strand by strand, the snarl comes undone and the burr releases its grip. Pulling on a burr just entangles it in the hair even more and makes a dog growly." Here's another secret: Give your dog tasty treats every few minutes during this grueling grooming session, and follow up with a thorough combing, brushing, and/or de-shedding session.

THE BATHROOM AS A SAFE HAVEN

Many pets seek out the bathroom when they are feeling overheated or stressed, or both at the same time. Because the room is mostly composed of cool porcelain between the tiles and the basins, it offers a convenient place for animals to chill out, literally. Cats especially love curling up in sinks, provided the faucet doesn't drip. In that case, they'll perch sinkside and use the faucet as their personal drinking fountain! Forget bud vases and the like—to me, nothing is as beautifully ornamental as a feline by the sink.

Pets with phobias of loud, sudden noises—like my Chow-Rottweiler mix Tiki, a sweet cowardly lion whom you wouldn't expect would be fearful of anything given his own intimidating appearance!—view the bathroom as a safe haven. If thunder and lightning are in the weather forecast, or you're expecting man-made pyrotechnics on Independence Day, by all means leave the bathroom door open so overwhelmed pets can go in there, lie down, and try to relax. I call this the "paw-celain" nesting instinct!

Like Princess here, my black cat Huey is a seasoned sink sitter, and he has me well trained: I always squeeze the tap handles tight to ensure that the faucet won't drip on his parade.

Provide Emergency Water

Never mind what the etiquette guidebooks and feng shui experts say about leaving the toilet seat down: In a dog residence, the toilet seat should always stay up because, in an emergency, it offers a vital supply of water to a thirsty canine tall enough to drink from it. Of course, for the safety of pets drinking out of the bowl, the toilet bowl must be kept free of any toxic chemical cleaners (for more on the topic of toilet safety, see chapter 9). And for obvious aesthetic reasons, the bowl should be kept spotless with daily swishes of natural cleaning supplies (for more on that topic, see chapter 7).

The Bathroom as Tropic Zone

Dogs and cats appreciate the bathroom's cooling properties, but parrots prefer the bathroom when it's steamy. Their natural habitat is the rain forest, after all, so hot, humid conditions in the bathroom, postshower, approximate that enormous natural sauna where they feel most at home. By all means bring birds into the bathroom to hang out; towel racks and shower-curtain bars can double as handy perches!

Parrots such as Angel, a rescued Cockatoo, enjoy hanging out in a steamy bathroom, where shower rods double as convenient perches. After her human housemates have taken a hot shower, the humidity in the bathroom simulates the tropical climate of a parrot's natural habitat: the rain forest.

Pretty Pet-Friendly

6

Groom Your Room

The only drawback to loving animals—apart from certain species' way-too-short life spans—is that you wind up wearing the evidence of your passion all over your clothing. Just as pets have a way of coming off on your wardrobe, leaving entire forests of shedded fur in their wake, they also come off on your furniture and your car's interior. Then you sit down, and your backside winds up as hairy as your front! Before I figured out how to combat all that shedded hair, on bad days I'd get lots of bemused looks and unsolicited comments such as, "You must have cats!" or "You're a dog lover, aren't you?"

I adore my animals, but I don't believe I have to wear that love on my sleeve—or on my coat or trouser legs, for that matter. Cutting down on shedded hair in the home is an important part of keeping the atmosphere hygienic. There's a novelty coffee mug I've seen that sports the legend, "Everything tastes better with dog hair in it." But I couldn't disagree more.

As animal lovers, we need to do everything we can to eliminate the evidence of excess pet hair so that we don't find it floating in our food and drink. Combating shedded pet hair does more than contribute to a clean, pleasant atmosphere at home; it can help you keep a low profile if you live in an apartment building, by preventing the migration of hairs from your place to the common areas, most of which are carpeted (and as you saw in chapter 1, carpets are a prime pet-hair magnet).

Keeping things neat also has other ramifications. Every time we leave our pet residences we become, knowingly or not, ambassadors for all pet owners. A lot of people already laugh at animal people, dismissing us as so many nuts, and this does nothing to advance the cause of shelter pet adoption. Eliminating the evidence of shedded hairs helps you look spiffy, and in so doing sends the message that having a pet doesn't have to mean looking slovenly.

With any luck, if more people see the stylish side of pet ownership, they'll go out and adopt a shelter pet for themselves. As animal lovers, there's absolutely no reason we shouldn't feel perfectly comfortable inviting guests in—without worrying that they'll emerge coated in dog and cat hairs. For the sake of the literally millions of dogs and cats awaiting homes at animal shelters across our country, I hope you'll join me in grooming your room—who knows, it could save a life or two!

PAW-PRINT PREVENTION

Chapter 1 discusses pet residences with a strict no-shoes policy. Because pets wear shoes only occasionally, you need to remove whatever mud or other form of filth they've collected on their paw pads before said filth has a chance to tattoo itself all over your floors and furnishings. The easiest way to do this is to keep nontoxic paw-wipes handy near your entryway and make a habit of using them when the need arises (don't overdo it). Make sure the brand of wipes you choose contains only botanical ingredients and no alcohol (which is drying to the paw-pad skin and could result in painful fissures). There are a few excellent products on the market designed just for pets, and one that's fine for pets and people to share when doing mitt decontamination; the latter is made by CleanWell, inventors of nontoxic antimicrobial products whose active ingredient is a botanical blend called Ingenium (read about it in chapter 7).

In the winter, if you live in a city where ice-melting salt is scattered on every sidewalk and roadway (and that's pretty much every city), the paw prints will be white or grayish in color—and in addition to irritating and even burning your dog's paw pads, the ice-melter also corrodes your floors. One way to prevent Spot's paws from exposure to this corrosive stuff is to outfit him or her with booties. However, certain dogs simply will not tolerate booties (my Angus is one of them). In that case, you'll need to put a protective coating of paw balm on his pads—and you'll need to wipe that off upon re-entering your home so that it doesn't leave prints all over the place.

Ever notice how, on a snowy or rainy day, it's not just Spot's paw pads that get splattered with filth, it's the dog's entire foreleg? I used to stage towels and bowls of warm water by my entry, so I'd be ready to give my dogs' legs a dunking. Of course, muddy water got spilled all over the place, necessitating even more cleanup. Happily, there's a great new invention to help you give Spot a quick paw-bath: the Paw Plunger. Just insert Spot's spotty legs, then remove them—along with whatever grime has attached itself to your dog's limbs.

Foot Note

Be aware that your own shoes can pick up particles of tracked litter, no matter what style of litter you use. With every step you take, the particles become pulverized into dust, and tracked wherever you go. I realized this when I noticed pale beige footprints on the dark hallway carpet of my apartment building: my own tracks. So now I'm very careful to remove my shoes before doing litter detail—or slip on zoris that I only wear indoors.

Escape Claws

Nail care is an important part of grooming a dog or cat, and ensuring pets' nails are kept short helps to keep your interior looking well-groomed, too. Stiletto-sharp cat claws can leave their mark on everything from the floors and walls to the fabric-covered furnishings, not to mention other pets, so blunting them with a careful clipping will help keep your décor from looking rough around the edges. (Don't even think about declawing a cat to preserve your furniture—it's cruel and unacceptable.) Happily, there are many clipping tools available that are professional quality, yet easy to use, making this sometimes onerous task as fast and simple as possible, for both you and your pet.

HAIRY SITUATION

Keeping shedded hair from overtaking your life involves mastering a balancing act between grooming your pets and grooming your interior. It goes without saying that in a pet residence, a powerful vacuum is a necessity. But vacuuming is hard work—and a joyless, thankless task—so the more you can reduce the amount of it you do, the more time you'll have left over to actually spend quality time with your pets. So even before you consider the V word, let's look at ways to cut down on shedded hair so you'll have less vacuuming to do.

Humidity is your friend when it comes to reducing shedded pet hairs—or any other hairs. (Let's not forget that we humans "shed," too, in dry weather.) Make sure your place doesn't become too dry, because very dry air saps a pet's coat (and a person's skin) of moisture, causing more hair to shed. Picture a Christmas tree a month or two after the holiday has come and gone: The drier the tree becomes, the more pine needles drop off it. The same happens to the individual hairs in a pet's coat, so it's important to keep the air in your pet residence from becoming too dry.

The low-tech way to add humidity to your space is by putting pots of water or cast-iron steamers near heat sources (such as wood stoves or radiators); as the water evaporates, it will humidify the air. The higher-tech solution, of course, is to plug in a humidifier, which will distribute humidity more efficiently through your space. If you're going to do that, select a humidifier with a handsome profile, one that you don't mind looking at while it sits around doing its thing.

Whether your pet wears long hair or short, and whether she has a double or single coat, keeping the fur moisturized from within and without is key to reducing shedding. Moisturizing from the inside, with oils, is discussed in chapter 4, and conditioning a pet's skin and coat topically is explained in chapter 5. In addition, regularly brushing and combing pets can go a long way toward preventing an excessively hairy interior (not to mention cutting down on your vacuuming time).

After a thorough brushing, my sable Border Collie, Sheba, produces enough wool—literally, a lawn-and-leaf bag full—to make me suspect she's not actually a dog, but one of the sheep her breed was designed to herd (hence her nickname, Sheepa). The idea of her luxurious red hairs being used by industrious birds to build their nests makes me smile, but finding those same hairs lodged in my salad dressing, floating in my beverages, and getting stuck under my tongue is much less appealing.

Happily, recent inventions in grooming products make it easier and faster than ever to remove excess hairs from dog and cat coats before those hairs can magnetically attach themselves to every surface of your home. These grooming tools are especially helpful if, like my Sheba, your dog wears a permanent double coat (you can tell if your dog is double-coated if, when you comb back the top hairs, you reveal a differently textured underlayer of hair, which in a double coat is much finer). One is a hybrid towel and rubber brush with flexible bristles that loosens about-to-shed hairs while providing an enjoyable massage. Especially useful are the tools that thin out a double coat's fine, downy underlayer—these, incidentally, are the hairs that are hardest to vacuum up, because they stick like Krazy Glue to any surface they come in contact with. Plus, thinning out the undercoat prevents matting as well as shedding. Just one short brushing session with either of my two fuzzy dogs, Sheba and Tiki, yields a bag full of fur per dog. Because the dogs' hairs are biodegradable, I'd hate to put them in a plastic bag that isn't, so I dispose of shedded hairs and other household detritus in biodegradable bags.

A Clean Sweep

Now that you're well versed in all the low-tech tools that will help you win the war against dust and shedded hair, it's time to bring out the big gun: a high-tech vacuum cleaner. Nature may abhor a vacuum, but pet residences can't stay clean without at least one powerful vacuum cleaner. Consequently, people living in pet residences adore a vacuum—and if they don't, they need to acquire one they can love, pronto. The brilliant inventor James Dyson made history—and his fortune—by designing the first bagless vacuum cleaner that doesn't lose suction. He told me that what motivated him were the years he spent living with two Golden Retrievers and facing the challenge of cleaning up their shedded hairs (he now has cats). I'm not surprised, are you?

The way a vacuum looks is important. I almost never get a chance to put my cool-looking, Jetsonesque, purple Dyson Animal Vacuum away in a closet because I use it so often that it has became part of the scenery at my pet residence. Happily, my cute pet vacuum is good-looking and, with its retractable hose "tail," compact enough that—although I would never say it "blends right in"—it's perfectly acceptable to keep it on display. Only half-jokingly, I described my Dyson to Mary Beth Breckenridge, reporter for the *Akron Beacon-Journal,* like this: "It has become part of the family. It's another pet."

Obviously, I'm not alone in making my vacuum cleaner a semipermanent part of my décor, because Dyson isn't the only manufacturer churning out stylish-looking machines that are as easy on the eyes as they are simple to use. For quick cleanup jobs, it helps to have a dedicated handheld vacuum cleaner that you can deploy at a moment's notice for a specific area in your home—such as the bed, where particles of cat litter often get tracked on kitty's paws. And of late, these fun little vacs have a lot of style, thanks to some truly creative product designers. There's even a vacuum that's the housekeeping equivalent of a light saber, emitting UV beams to terminate dust mites! The new breed of vacuum cleaners look like cool toys, which actually helps motivate some kids to want to use them to clean up their rooms.

Still, it's funny how even the most high-tech of vacuum cleaners have a way of taking on that distinctively stale vacuum cleaner smell. Fragranced vacuum beads, available at stores and online, are a great way to make the chore of sweeping more fun and less onerous. Before suctioning, scatter the beads on the floor; your machine's airflow will activate the odor neutralizer. (For safety, leave pets out of the room so they don't vacuum up the beads before you do.) Or, scatter some dried lavender or peppermint leaves, and suck those up as you go along. Okay, so it's not exactly aromatherapy, but the hint of fragrance helps you get the job done without scowling—and keeps the vacuum smelling more pleasant as it sits while not in use.

If you're going to flout the no-rug rule (see chapter 1) by living with rugs and/or carpeting, make sure you select a machine designed for the specific task of suctioning hairs from carpets, one that has a powerful beater brush, such as the Felix by Sebo. To take care of messes on the carpet that were once wet and have now dried, environmentally friendly cleaning techniques are discussed in chapter 7. If you have a pet who is prone to frequent accidents, or you've moved into a carpeted home where other people's pets lived, consider investing in a black light to illuminate trouble spots (dried urine glows under black light). This way, you can rest assured you've thoroughly cleaned those spots, so they won't attract animals to re-mark over them.

To clean traces of Jurassic liquids or solids from carpets, use liquid cleaners (as discussed in chapter 7) or solid ones such as Odorzout or Clear the Air, formulated specifically for cat urine. The active ingredients of these granular cleaning products are minerals that absorb and trap odors. Sprinkle the granules onto a carpeted surface, let them sit for several hours per the directions on the package, and then vacuum them up. You may need to reapply several times until all odors are—well—out! With each application, please don't forget to close pets out of the room so that they won't do the vacuuming for you with their snouts, resulting in an emergency trip to the vet.

If you're lucky enough to catch a hairball soon after it's been deposited on a carpet, before the tossed stomach juices have a chance to seep all the way into the rug fibers, here's a natural solution: Lift up the solid part of the mess, pour baking soda over the rest, and leave it to dry. The baking soda granules will absorb the icky stuff, enabling you to vacuum it out of the carpet.

Vac Attack

If your pets appear terrorized by the vacuum cleaner, cowering in fear or barking vehemently at the thing, do the kind thing and close them in another room. There's no need to stress out your extra-sensitive pets as you try to erase evidence of their shedded hairs. Look at it from the animals' perspective: Here's this loud monster that keeps barreling around unpredictably, sometimes even in their direction, all the while sucking up everything that crosses its path. Yikes! Understandably, pets view the rolling suction machine as a dangerous intruder. The low-to-the-ground Roomba robotic vacuum has become legendary for unknowingly provoking fights with all sorts of house pets as it goes about its programmed business. The Roomba

The Cleaning Pros Weigh In

"Nobody outcleans THE MAIDS"—that's the bold slogan of THE MAIDS Home Services, a residential cleaning franchise serving more than forty states and four provinces in Canada. These cleaning pros share two valuable tips for depilating your interior:

- If you have a dog or cat that sheds like crazy, check out vacuum attachments with rubber strips.
- When removing pet hair from draperies, carpets, and upholstery, the vacuum is not always your best weapon. Use a rubber latex glove, wet or dry, to do the job, because pet hair will cling to it.

To those tips, add this one: A great way to pick up shedded pet hairs from any fabric surface is with a clean dryer sheet. This makes perfect sense, as dryer sheets cut down on static, and static is what causes pet hairs to cling stubbornly to fabrics. However, please take care to use an eco-friendly dryer sheet such as Method Home's softener infused dryer cloths (for more on green cleaning products, see chapter 7), as the cationic detergents present in other fabric softeners and dryer sheets can cause serious health problems in pets, including pulmonary edema and kidney failure, according to the *Merck Veterinary Manual*. Also, never, ever use a dryer sheet directly on a pet, and don't let them use the sheets as toys. This advice comes from a reliable source: Debi Romano of Save Kitty, an excellent nonprofit cat rescue group. Debi has an advantage on many of us in the cleaning department: For many years, she cleaned people's homes professionally, and now dedicates her time to rescuing cats, so she's better qualified than almost anyone to give advice on grooming a pet residence. Another weapon Debi deploys in the battle against shedded hair is 3M's Fur Fighter, which comes with a microfiber pad that may be vacuumed and reused as often as necessary.

doesn't seek out confrontation, but its presence is enough to annoy many dogs, who view the vac as a persistent intrusion on their personal space that must be stopped. The anecdotes from pet owners were compelling enough to merit a feature article on the subject in no less prestigious a publication than the *Wall Street Journal!*

EAT MY DUST

Dusting is a drag, so arm yourself with cheerful, stylish tools such as colorful telescoping dusters that will get your cats' attention. If you're game, you'll find that your cats—clever creatures that they are—will turn dusting into a contact sport, swatting at the duster as you drag it along high shelves and wall moldings, over the table and under the bed. One of the things that inspired me to write this book was the quality time I spent multitasking with my beloved cat Ludmilla, who appointed herself my dusting motivator. Later, when Ludmilla developed liver disease, it became more important to me than ever to keep her quarters as clean as they could be, to prevent health complications, so I was grateful for her playful supervision.

Believe it or not, shedded pet hairs actually make the chore of dusting go faster. Dust on the floor has a way of making itself hard to see—until, that is, your mother comes over for a visit, at which point dust steps into the spotlight and practically screams to make itself known. But one great advantage to keeping pets is that they actually help you get an edge in the endless war against dust. The hairs they inevitably shed and the dust that's inescapable are magnetically attracted to each other, forming formidable dust bunnies that are easy to spot from across the room, so you can scoop them up well before any hypercritical VIP visitor makes a visit to your place.

A dustpan and brush is an old-fashioned tool, indeed, but recent incarnations boast ergonomic rubber handles, cheerful colors, and clever designs, so you'll actually want to keep them around and use them. Don't overwork your vacuum cleaner by having it suck up huge amounts of tracked litter; sweep those into the dustpan before you start running the vacuum. Also, for middle-of-the-night or early-morning accidents, when the noise of a vacuum isn't an option (if you live in an apartment building), a dustpan is a necessity. Later, don't forget to vacuum the brush, though, because superfine cat hairs have a tendency to stick to the bristles.

Even a bummer of a chore like dusting can be a great opportunity for quality bonding time with your pets. My beautiful cat Ludmilla enjoyed swatting at the telescoping duster I use to wipe down the cat shelves and other hard-to-reach surfaces in my home.

Speaking of tracked litter, you can help cut down on it significantly by placing a rubber mat in front of your cat's box, designed expressly for the purpose of catching litter granules from cats' paws before they can be tracked all over your home. You'll need to shake that mat out every day and sweep underneath and around the box. Need incentive? Here it is: Tracked litter usually winds up in the bed—your bed—so using a mat will prevent yet another cleanup duty (and you'll sleep more comfortably without those "kitty crumbs").

CLOTHES CALL

Chapter 3 examines performance upholstery fabric options that resist the difficult tendency of pet hairs—especially the quill-like hairs of short-coated dogs—to weave their way through a woven or knit fabric. When selecting your wardrobe, remember that some materials used in the manufacture of clothing attract more pet hairs than others, too. Ever notice how you'll lint-roll a cotton T-shirt or wool knit sweater—and then lift the sweater to find that many of

Tacky, Tacky (in a Good Way)

Tape hair-lifters are a necessity to keep on hand if you live with more than one pet of any species. Be a good host and hand them to departing guests on their way out; they may not be aware of just how much hair they've picked up on a brief visit to your place even if you thought it was spotless. If you want to be a *great* host, grab a lint roller and roll your guests' backsides for them! Also, it's a good idea to keep one roller in your handbag or briefcase, and another in your car, so you're always prepared to roll stray pet hairs off your clothing. This comes in especially handy if you've got reservations at a nice restaurant and you want to avoid being seated by the bathroom.

Happily, the concept of the lint roller has extended to housekeeping products, so it's now possible to buy long-handled rollers (the adhesive equivalent of a paint roller) as well as large (23-inch × 35-inch) sheets of sticky tape for large, hairy surfaces. Before you expect company, simply place these sheets on the sofa, bedspread, or wherever you suspect a major hair problem, and then peel away the hair. You'll be truly slack-jawed to see how much hair was there. The edges of the tape sheets can squeeze into tight sofa crevices, such as the welting of your upholstery and other hair traps. I always think of this as a Brazilian wax for the sofa!

the hairs you thought you'd removed had merely migrated to the other side? In a vicious cycle, you sit down on your sofa while wearing hairy clothes, and . . . you get the picture.

As with upholstery materials, if you don't want to look like you rolled out of a kennel, you'll want to select garments made of tightly woven fabrics. In recent years, I've found myself gravitating to spiffy cotton button-down shirts because the tight weave resists pet hairs a lot better than other shirts, and because the shirts require ironing to look their best. As a result, I tend to be better dressed and more professional-looking than when I wore T-shirts—so avoiding shedded hairs has been good for my image!

At the other end of the textile spectrum, Polarfleece is one of my favorite materials for cold-weather wear (and dog bed covers), but it does attract pet hairs, especially cat hairs, like a magnet—an effect that's compounded in winter by the natural phenomenon known as static cling, which makes pet hairs hang on with remarkable tenacity even in the face of a dependably sticky lint-roller or powerful vacuum. I happen to wear lots of Polarfleece to walk my dogs when temperatures dip—my fleece separates keep me so comfortable and warm that I don't have to cut short the dogs' winter walk time. But I also expect my Polarfleece items to multitask, as I will often combine the sleeker-looking black Polarfleece leggings with dressier jackets, coats, and heels. So to save myself extra cleanup effort, I'm careful to remove those thermally efficient togs before communing with my cats, as I'll invariably end up looking a mess—and having a hell of a time removing those cat hairs from my fleece garments.

I'm also careful to reserve a pair of shoes exclusively for wearing to the dog park, where I know they'll wind up caked with mud on the outside, filled with sand on the inside, and generally unpresentable outside the company of fellow dog-lovers!

THE LEASH YOU CAN DO

If you have multiple dogs, containing the leashes, harnesses, and other needful items goes a long way to keeping your home looking well groomed—especially if certain humans in your household, ahem, have trouble remembering where they left the leashes after a particularly early-morning or late-night outing with the dogs. There's really nothing worse than leaving leashes on the floor or draped over chairs. Besides the clutter factor, you may come home to find them chewed beyond recognition. A leash rack or coat rack helps to rein in all those tethers, cuts down on disorganization and destruction, and helps the forgetful humans in your house (they know who they are) remember where to find the leashes.

PICK OF THE LITTER

A cat's loo is an item that, if not selected and displayed with care, can seriously detract from a home's aesthetic atmosphere, causing it to appear less than glamorous. Having a good-looking arrangement is especially important if you have more than one cat, as the rule is at least one box (or two) per cat. And yet, for many years, cat lovers had few if any options in the aesthetic litter box department: The cat box was a box and nothing more, usually a plastic rectangle in a nondescript shade of beige. Today, happily, there are plenty of manufacturers thinking outside the box to create high-style cat comfort stations, some so cleverly camouflaged that they needn't be relegated to a basement bathroom. Plus, certain designs even provide the handy solution of a pocket for stowing the scoop so it's not laying around on the floor.

I'm not big into plants—I'm just not good at keeping flora alive, and besides, there are simply too many plant species that are toxic to pets (for more information on that topic, see chapter 9). So I keep things simple: The only live plants at my place are boxes of organic wheatgrass, purchased from my local farmer's market, for the cat and dogs to nibble at. But thanks to the Hidden Litter Planter, I can have what looks like a tall, majestic plant, but is in fact a clever and decorative cat loo. The eye is drawn up toward the green leaves of the "plant" and away from the actual box.

With any litter box, you have a big question to answer: To cover the cat box or not to cover the cat box? A closed box affords a cat more privacy, but at the same time, it also restricts her view of her surroundings—and many cats have an instinctive need for a 360-degree vista while they eliminate. Your parlor panthers may be domesticated, but they possess the souls of tigers—and in the wild, tigers don't like to feel vulnerable to attack by predators while heeding nature's call.

But the choice of an open or covered box is not really yours—it's your cat's. Kitty will vote with her feet as to what style of box she prefers, and a good way to find out is to offer her one open style and one closed, and see which gets used more (some brands are convertible, so you can leave the top off for a high-walled open box if it turns out Kitty prefers the open style). In terms of the box's other features, that's your call, but keep in mind that two criteria will ensure that you have less cleanup to do in the long run. A good box should have high walls, even if it's topless, to keep droppings from dripping over the sides. It should also be big enough for your cat—providing a too-small box is asking for extra cleanup work. As the great American architect Louis Sullivan said, "Form follows function." It pays to keep that credo top of mind when making cat loo arrangements.

Happily, there are plenty of high-style options in litter boxes, with cheerful colors and patterns. But without a doubt, the most high-style solution for concealing what every cat owner prefers to hide is the Kattbank. The Swedish word for "cat bench," Kattbank is the invention of designers Travis Weedman and Arielle Glade, married principals of the design firm Compressed Pattern in Portland, Oregon. For house-proud cat lovers, especially those living in small spaces, their creation is the biggest design scoop since Ed Lowe of Michigan invented cat litter in 1947. Kattbank is a ventilated seat that's an effective litter-cloaking device. To test it, Weedman and Glade invited friends over for dinner—and their guests didn't guess that they were sitting pretty on a kitty toilet!

What's more, Kattbank has a sleek profile that has earned it coverage in such magazines as *Time, Metropolitan Home*, and *I.D.* Made of hardwood plywood and finished in your choice of wood veneer or color lacquer, Kattbank comes in two lengths: 48 inches (for one cat) or 60 inches (long enough to accommodate two cats). The bottom of the bench is lined with a removable plastic grid that cleans a cat's paws as she exits, so litter won't get tracked all over your place. Of course, revolutionary design does not come cheap: The Kattbank's retail price is in the four figures.

SWEET SMELL OF . . . FERRETS?

Nothing spoils the look of a pet residence more than the way it smells—even the loveliest pet-friendly pad loses pretty points if the atmosphere is such that you need to pinch your nose shut upon entering. Chapter 8 discusses ways to improve the air quality in your pet residence. In the meantime, if you live with cats (or any other species that utilizes litter, such as rabbits or ferrets), vigilance is your best atmospheric deodorant: Be on the ball about monitoring litter boxes several times daily, and scoop whenever you see a new development.

Even small pets can produce gigantic odors. If your child keeps a "pocket pet"—a hamster or gerbil, say—cage vigilance is key to stay on top of things that need picking up. Unpleasant odors come not just from droppings, but from uneaten lettuce and other foods that spoil quickly. Don't use deodorizing bedding, as it can be toxic; cedar shavings, for instance, contain fragrant oils that can irritate small pets, causing respiratory or liver problems. Bedding made from corncobs is also to be avoided, as it promotes the growth of mold and fungus.

The best bedding/litter options for small pets are phenol-free and made of hemp or cellulose fiber. Rabbits are notorious for nibbling at absolutely everything, including their own litter and bedding, so be sure that what you provide them with is safely edible.

7

Green Clean

Many people believe that only harsh, nose-wrinkling chemicals have true cleaning power. But pleasantly fragrant botanical oils are actually quite powerful—if you don't believe me, try pouring straight lavender oil on a painted surface, leave it for a few minutes, and watch the paint start to dissolve and peel! There are so many toxic chemicals we're exposed to on a daily basis that there's really no reason to use toxic chemicals to keep our homes clean. Pets, being smaller than we are, tend to be much more vulnerable to the adverse health effects of those toxic chemicals. And there's no reason to punish the environment with toxic chemicals every time we clean.

The great news is that every single surface in your home, hard or soft, can be cleaned in an eco-friendly green way, without sacrificing hygiene in the least. For every cleaner you can name, there's a nontoxic alternative that is equally efficient, if not more so. In chapter 5, I discussed some toxic chemicals that should be avoided in personal grooming products, for both pets and people; those same toxic chemicals happen to be the key ingredients of most mass-produced household cleaners. It takes little effort to select brands that are safe, so for the sake of your pets and all the other members of your family, please make that effort.

GREENING THE CLEAN FOR PET HEALTH

Animals experience the world not just with their noses and eyes but with their tongues. Pets lick things—yes, even things that gross out us humans—to register important information. By using nontoxic, environmentally safe, and biodegradable cleaning products made from natural ingredients, pet owners can rest easy that Spot and friends are not ingesting trace amounts of harmful chemicals by licking at surfaces cleaned with them. And these products are every bit as effective—yes, even an eco-friendly drain cleaner (it's called Earthworm)—so there is absolutely no need to buy poisonous products.

How you clean your wood floors is of particular importance. For wood floors with no paint on them, you can maintain their luster even in the wake of a nasty accident or two without using wood wax that contains toluene or other toxic chemicals. You won't be sacrificing your floor's good looks by protecting your pets from exposure to toxic waxes. Clean and condition trouble spots simultaneously with a nontoxic wood cleaner such as Method Home's Wood for Good. Where a deeper conditioning is needed, use Farmhouse Furniture Wax (a delightfully fragrant blend of carnauba wax and lavender oil) or, if you have bamboo floors, Bamboo Goo. With these products, you can rest easy when you notice your cat licking at the floor.

A fringe benefit of eco-friendly products is that they proudly state on the package that they are not tested on animals, the way that mass brands often are. No true animal lover wants to support companies that willingly conduct—or hire others to conduct—cruel tests on innocent animals. So that you can be a fully informed shopper, request a list of companies that test on animals by contacting the National Anti-Vivisection Society (www.navs.org).

EASY (ON THE NOSE) BEING GREEN

Using green cleaners is also important in a pet residence because animals' sense of smell is exquisitely fine-tuned; they can smell things we can't, detecting, say, a whiff of Jurassic urine that our nostrils can't pick up because it has been masked with a heavily fragranced household cleaner. If we mere humans find the scent of certain chemical household cleaners offensive, imagine how our animals feel. In fact, we don't need to imagine it; pets register their discomfort by sneezing when they pick up the scent of those chemical-laden cleaners, because they come across as an assault on their delicate sniffers. Like children, animals are much smaller than we are, making them even more vulnerable to the ravages of hazardous chemicals.

Living in a pet residence, you are bound to do a lot more cleaning than if you were petless. And frankly, whether you have pets or not, if you've just undertaken a monumental cleaning task—say, spring cleaning—you can easily tire of the scent of your green cleaner, no matter how lovely it smells. Believe me, this is a major downer, and one that contributes to housekeeping procrastination. For example, I happen to adore Sun & Earth's all-purpose cleaner, with its fresh orange-coconut scent, partly because it was one of the first eco-friendly

Seventh Generation is part of the core group of green cleaners I use every day on a rotating basis. I like to key different scents to different rooms in the home—delicious cucumber for the kitchen; restful lavender for the bedroom and bath.

cleaners on the market that was easy to find in stores. But after using it all the time, every day, for several years, my brain suffered fragrance fatigue—I began to equate its citrus scent with the foul stuff it was erasing. I still use Sun & Earth, but now I rotate my cleaning products, using specific ones for different rooms. So, in the kitchen, I'll use Parsley Power or Method Home Cucumber or Grapefruit, because I love the idea of cleaning cooking and food-prep surfaces with an herb, vegetable, or fruit that is also an ingredient in delicious cuisine.

SURFACE-SPECIFIC CLEANING PRODUCTS

Years ago, cleaning house was a lot more traumatic for those of us who hate housekeeping— especially for the chemically sensitive among us—because the only cleaning products available on the market were toxic chemical brews with industrial-strength fragrances that stank to heaven. (I'm not going to mention names, but I think you know the loud smells I'm referring to.) Those toxic chemical brews are still the most widely available on the market but, happily, consumers are becoming more and more educated about which ingredients to avoid, as well as the tremendous benefits of going green.

When environmentally friendly (a.k.a. "green") cleaners appeared on the scene—touting no toxic ingredients and lighter, more natural scents—they were hard to get in stores; one had to practically be a detergent detective to find them. Today, we have a full menu of choices when it comes to green-cleaning products, and the natural alternatives have become so popular that they're widely available in stores. There's a good reason green cleaners are in demand: They really work—in many cases, much more effectively than their chemical-laden counterparts.

 ■ **Floors**   Because pets spend a lot of their time on the floor, green cleaners are a necessity for swabbing your decks even if you don't use them for any other application. Still, exercise caution by closing pets out of the room until the floors are dry so they won't lick at the cleaner or absorb it through their paw pads.

- **Glass**   The skin on moist schnozzes absorbs chemicals frightfully easily, so avoid glass cleaners containing ammonia; green cleaners whose key ingredient is vinegar are much kinder to pets, and they work just as well to erase evidence of slobbery snouts pressed up against glass (something all pets love to do), whether it's a window or a mirror.

- **Tile**   Why not clean the ceramic surfaces in your bathroom with the pleasantly Ylang-Ylang–scented Daily Shower spray cleaner by Method Home?

- **Paint**   Go easy on walls and other painted surfaces, because even green spray cleaners can melt away the color, especially if the paint contains volatile organic compounds (for more on paint, see chapter 2). To wipe away messes, use a cloth or sponge dampened with warm water.

- **Wood**   Furniture is best cleaned with a nontoxic wood cleaner that will condition the wood, such as Wood for Good by Method Home. This product also works well on wood floors, but if a deeper, more conditioning clean is needed, use a thicker product such as Farmhouse Furniture Wax or, if you have bamboo flooring, Bamboo Goo.

- **Plastic litter box**   Don't use any detergent with a strong scent—in fact, it's best not to use any detergent at all, as the scent could deter Kitty from using the box. Wash litter boxes with hot, hot water—that's all. If you must use detergent, try cleaning one box with an unscented green laundry detergent as a test; rinse thoroughly, and if Kitty accepts her box after all is washed and dried, you know it's okay to use going forward. (For more on this subject, see chapter 8.)

- **Concrete**   As you discovered in chapter 5, many shampoos for pets and people contain enough sulfates to double as effective concrete cleaners. So don't buy a super-harsh garage-floor-cleaning product for this purpose; just use ordinary shampoo, instead.

I'm not saying that cleaning is a joy or a desirable pastime, but with green cleaners it certainly doesn't have to be a dreaded chore that leaves you choking, coughing, sneezing, or watery-eyed. That was how I used to feel using those old-fashioned cleaning products. No wonder I diligently avoided cleaning! Now, I've grown so accustomed to gentle-yet-effective green cleaners that when I enter environments that were cleaned with old-fashioned, industrial-strength cleaning products, I can tell the difference immediately because my eyes water and I start sneezing. And I usually try to get out of there fast.

IN THE KITCHEN: CHIEF COOK AND BOTTLE WASHER

While you're in the kitchen, give a moment's pause to the matter of washing dinnerware—your own and Spot's. If you've got a dishwasher, it's a simple matter to keep everything clean (and please use a green brand of dishwashing detergent, such as Seventh Generation). But if, like me, you're still stuck washing dishes by hand (here's a bit of trivia for you: The handsome actor Willem Dafoe loves doing dishes at dinner parties), please don't use sponges treated with harsh germicidal chemicals for your own dishes or Spot's. Always opt for natural cellulose sponges, preferably recycled; some of these are backed with loofah for scrubbing efficiency. Extend the sponges' life the good, old-fashioned way, by keeping them dry (or as dry as possible) between uses and boiling them for a few minutes in a pot of water on the stove top.

To avoid cross-contamination if you don't have a dishwasher, keep the sponge you use for your own dishes separate from the one you use for Spot's bowls. I use a vintage sponge holder in the shape of a whale for my pet sponge, which really comes in handy when the sponges are the same color. As for dishwashing liquid, green is the way to go so that pets don't ingest traces of chemical cleaners when they take a drink or eat their meals.

The harsh chemical used in synthetic sponges to retard bacterial growth is the antibacterial and antifungal agent triclosan, which is also a key ingredient of most hand sanitizers, hand soaps, and dishwashing detergents on the market. Triclosan is registered with the Environmental Protection Agency as a pesticide; however, a U.S. Food and Drug Administration advisory

Pretty Pet-Friendly

committee found that household use of antibacterial products provides no benefits over soap and water, while the American Medical Association recommends that triclosan not be used in the home, as it may encourage bacterial resistance to antibiotics. Triclosan is linked to liver and inhalation toxicity, and it's also a potent endocrine disruptor, messing with the thyroid and unbalancing the sex hormones estrogen and androgen. (Chemicals that disrupt sex hormones have been implicated in breast cancer and the early onset of puberty.)

Here's more bad news about triclosan for those who love animals and care about the environment: Triclosan is believed to destroy fragile aquatic ecosystems, especially algae that other animals may depend on, either directly or indirectly. Sewage and wastewater treatment plants cannot remove triclosan, so the compound remains stable for a long time, posing an increasing problem in our waterways. Sadly, it's one of the most common man-made chemicals found in U.S. streams.

I wash my hands dozens of times in an average day—what with all the dog-walking I do (I use biodegradable poop-scoop bags, which are not entirely nonporous), not to mention all the additional cat-litter-scooping—and the majority of my hand-washing happens in the kitchen sink. To be certain I'm not exposing myself to triclosan while still ensuring that bacteria aren't traveling from my mitts to my mouth (and from my dogs' dishes to mine), I spritz with CleanWell, an all-natural, poison-free germicide made with Ingenium, a patented botanical formula that kills 99.99 percent of germs, including MRSA (*staphylococcus*), *E. coli,* and *salmonella* on contact. (Plus, CleanWell is also alcohol-free, so it doesn't dry oft-washed hands.)

One key ingredient of Ingenium happens to be thyme, used for centuries as a medicinal plant and antiseptic as well as a culinary herb, which makes it especially appropriate for use in the kitchen, where so many recipes call for that herb. CleanWell smells delightfully fresh and is poison-free and completely safe for kids; in fact, its creation was inspired by a boy named Connor who was born with a compromised immune system. Connor's dad, Sam, collaborated with his mother, an aromacologist and a physician. As it happens, both Sam's family

When young Connor was born, his immune system functioned at only 10 percent. He's the inspiration for the creation of CleanWell, a poison-free antibacterial soap that his father, Sam, worked hard to develop. Without CleanWell, a pet might have been out of the question for Connor; happily, here he is with his Pug pal, Frankie.

and the doctor have dogs at home. It's likely that Connor wouldn't be able to live with a dog were it not for CleanWell, and any product that enables a boy and his dog to be together gets my two thumbs-up!

THE LIFT OF LAVENDER

In the bathroom, I like cleaning with products that smell like beauty and grooming products, such as Lifetree's Lavender-Tea Tree bathroom cleaner. In the bedroom, lavender is a great choice because of its calming, aromatherapeutic property—it's exactly the scent you want to inhale when you're trying to drift off to sleep. And it shows up in many green-cleaning products.

Lavender has become a cleaning staple in my home. I'm not talking about something infused with a lavender scent; I'm talking *Lavandula officinalis*, essential oil of lavender that you purchase at a health-food store. This is powerful stuff, and at about $7 per ounce, it doesn't come cheap. Thankfully, a few drops go a long way, as I learned by sprinkling lavender oil on my sheets and pillows, and in my bath water, to keep everything smelling nice. The great

Pretty Pet-Friendly

thing about lavender is that, like tea tree oil (*Melaleuca alternifolia* in Latin), it's also a natural flea deterrent, so it's ideal for freshening up dog beds in between laundry sessions, in case your best friend may have carried home an unwanted, parasitic guest at the dog park.

But it wasn't until I took my cats for an appointment with holistic veterinarian Dr. Gerald Buchoff of New Jersey that I learned the best reason of all to use lavender in cleanup applications. Not only does it smell wonderful, calm frazzled nerves, and repel fleas, but it's also a natural antiseptic. When one of my cats accidentally hooked a claw in the vet's hand, Dr. Buchoff immediately broke out a small glass bottle of lavender oil and dabbed it on the cut.

Not long after that, I had a bad day at home; while fostering a 6-month-old pup with spotty (literally) housetraining skills, I found myself out of green cleaners at the precise moment that I was faced with several quarts of urine, plus a dark brown monument on the wood floor near my front door. I had to improvise, and fast—I rent my apartment, so there's always a chance that someone will complain about "pet odor," real or imagined, and my landlord will begin eviction proceedings.

After scooping up the solid part of the mess, I spied my trusty little one-ounce bottle of essential lavender oil. I shook out a few drops, then poured a tall glass of steaming-hot tap water over the area to spread and dilute the oil, and finished by mopping it all up with paper towels. It's important not to let the straight oil sit on a painted or polyurethane-treated surface, because it is strong enough to melt off the finish.

This emergency concoction did the job beautifully. What's more, my place smelled like a health spa; I felt totally relaxed; I was confident that the germs were dead; and the wood floor was none the worse for wear because I'd cleaned it with oil, which conditioned the wood. That day, I supersized to a sixteen-ounce bottle, which I decant into one-ounce bottles to avoid spilling out too much of this precious oil at any one time. And ever since, I try to make sure I never run out of this pet-friendly cleaning "essential," staging a small bottle in every room.

I'm also convinced that my frequent use of calming lavender oil is what has enabled me to welcome so many foster dogs into my home—combined with Susan Raimond's famously calming harp music playing on the CD player, no one feels unduly stressed out, and so few spats erupt.

HANDLING AN EPIC ACCIDENT

Of course, if you've ever lived with animals, even just one, you know that a little pee and poop on a wood floor is a cakewalk compared to some other cleaning challenges that can arise when pets are your roommates. How about the time I returned home to discover that one of my senior dogs had eliminated on the bed? Thankfully, I caught it in time, so I was able to fold the comforter over on itself and lift it off the bed to spare the mattress. In my haste to stop the liquid matter from leaking through, however, I managed to smear the solid matter on the fabric. Nice!

What to do next? In the old days, I confess I would have done the wasteful thing and tossed that comforter in the trash as being just too icky. But rescuing animals gives one a new perspective on pollution and waste; rescue is a noble form of recycling, after all, and as long as you're recycling animals' lives, you may as well do your best to recycle wherever else you can. I was determined to try and salvage that comforter.

I consider myself very lucky that as a pets columnist, companies large and small send me products to road-test and share with my readers. But the thing that sets me apart from most of my colleagues is that I insist on testing out all products I write about before I recommend them to my readers! I'm not one to be swayed by fancy packaging, because I care about what's inside. (This is not something all pet product manufacturers appreciate, because too many of them emphasize style over substance.) On this day, one of the products awaiting road-testing was Get Serious, a nontoxic stain and odor extractor with a proprietary formula.

I grabbed the bottle along with my green laundry detergent and headed out the door in the direction of the Laundromat.

A quick word about green laundry detergent: It's the only kind I'll use, because pets have a habit of licking at sheets. I don't want them ingesting trace chemicals, so I never use detergents with optical brighteners and other toxic, nonbiodegradable ingredients—my favorite brands include Seventh Generation, Ecover, Ecos, Planet, and Vermont Soap's Liquid Sunshine; for really filthy laundry, Method Home 3X does the trick, even turning blackened towels white again. Also, many of my dogs have extremely sensitive skin, and one also has allergies, so I don't want to use towels on them that were washed in scary chemicals that could irritate them and cause them to scratch excessively. For the same reason, I stay away from chlorine bleach, so my white laundry stays that way with the addition of Ecover's Ecological Non-Chlorine Bleach Ultra to the washing machine.

Arriving at the Laundromat two blocks from my apartment, I laid the comforter on the sidewalk outside and pretreated all the affected areas with Get Serious, following the directions on the package and pretreating the parts that were—ahem—brown-streaked. Then I gathered up the object, gingerly placed it in an extra-large-capacity washing machine so it would have room to move and agitate itself clean, selected a hot water wash, added detergent plus one cup of Get Serious, put in my quarters, and watched the presoak cycle begin. Half an hour later, I was astonished to see—and smell—that the comforter really was as good as new. Get Serious also works miracles to remove olfactory (pheromones) and visual (stains) evidence from carpets and rugs.

If you think I'm eccentric for keeping no fewer than ten bottles of this product on hand at any given time, here's a true story that may convince you otherwise. In my hometown of New York City, when it's pouring rain or snowing, many ordinarily law-abiding citizens tend to flout the poop-scoop law, resulting in treacherous patches of liquid brown stuff just waiting to be tracked indoors where it doesn't belong. Unbeknownst to me, this misdemeanor took place one evening just a few short feet from the entrance to my apartment building while I was enjoying Japanese dinner out.

In short order, someone big and tall stepped in this pile and proceeded to stomp size-13 (or perhaps larger) shoe prints of excrement all over the gray broadloom carpet of my building's hallway, right outside my door (I live on the parlor floor). To say I was grossed out upon arriving home would be an understatement. And here's the best part: As the tenant with the pets, it doesn't take Alfred Hitchcock to figure out who would be the prime suspect. So it fell to me to clean up the mess before the landlord got a whiff of what had happened. Ugh!

Thankfully, I was armed that night with Get Serious, which works magic even on dried-up fecal matter that threatens to become indelible. Following the instructions on the bottle, I saturated (but didn't soak) all fourteen—count 'em, fourteen—sickening stains, and then blotted each one dry with paper towels, cursing all the way. The next morning, you could barely tell from the carpet that anything untoward had even happened—that's how well Get Serious works. But the real test came when my dogs walked past what had previously been a malodorous minefield and didn't even stop for a sniff. That's how you can really tell Get Serious is the s--- (and I mean that in the most complimentary way).

Get Serious also works brilliantly on urine, which is critical if you're housetraining a puppy who has had an accident or two. As we all know, dogs can detect the scent of urine that you think you've cleaned up, so be sure to extract the odor with Get Serious instead of just covering it up with something that smells good to you.

Years ago, my beloved cat Cyrus went into cardiac arrest during a routine procedure while under anesthesia. I'm convinced that while his brain was starved for oxygen, he sustained mild brain damage, because ever since, the poor creature occasionally misses the litter box—by a half-mile. One of his recent targets happened to be a really nice Ralph Lauren linen sweater, only I didn't discover this unfortunate development until a day or two after the fact, giving cat urine—one of the most offensive odors on earth—a chance to thoroughly permeate the garment. Unbelievably, after pretreating with Get Serious and two thorough hand-washings in cold water with Vermont Soap's Liquid Sunshine, the sweater no longer reeks of cat urine, and may be worn in polite society without attracting the olfactory attention of dogs, cats, or any other species.

After vintage cat urine, the second most offensive odor produced by animals is excreted by a pet's anal sacs after a bowel movement—but if there's a blockage, every once in a while, the anal sac will surprise-express itself, spritzing unpleasantness anywhere from your sofa to the backseat of your car. This is usually accompanied by butt-scooting, so if you notice your pet pitifully dragging around his rear end, you might be able to head off an involved cleanup session with Get Serious by bringing your pet to the vet to have the anal sacs expressed. But if it happens, it's a great relief to know that Get Serious will take care of smeared slipcovers, floors, and rugs.

8

Clearing the Air

The importance of fresh air cannot be overstated: You can have a living space designed by the most famous "starchitect," outfitted with all the latest, most expensive home furnishings, accessories, and high-tech gadgets. But if you can't take a deep breath at home without gagging, all those trappings amount to very little indeed.

CLEAN = UNSCENTED

In chapter 7, I waxed rhapsodic about Get Serious, a highly effective odor and stain extractor. This product is key to creating a clean, blank, odor-free slate in my pet residence. The reason it works so well is that it removes malodorous messes at the source instead of masking them (as many other products do). Masking offensive odors and stains might fool you and your human guests, but it won't fool your pets. And if the offending odor is urine, nothing will stop a dog from re-marking the spot.

Sometimes, a cat will bring up a hairball somewhere on your bed linens and you just won't notice it; then you'll throw it in the wash and wonder why the entire load of finished laundry smells funny—even if you used, say, Seventh Generation laundry detergent with its sweet scent of White Flower & Bergamot. (Or you might not notice the smell until bedtime, as you lay your head down on the just-washed pillowcase, and . . . eeew.) If that should happen, simply do the laundry over, this time pretreating the spot with Get Serious and also adding a cup to the washing machine. When the machine winds down after the final spin cycle, you'll notice a big difference in how fresh the laundry smells. I use this product periodically as a prewash for my clothing, just to be sure I'm not wearing a distinctive scent.

FOOLPROOF FENESTRATION

The window is the low-tech way to air out a room, but with smaller pets, it's critical that window frames be outfitted with sturdy, tight-fitting screens to prevent injuries and fatalities from "high rise syndrome," the sad phenomenon of cats leaping from tall windows in pursuit of birds, butterflies, or other winged creatures. Even with larger pets who won't try to jump out, it's worth the extra money to have custom ones installed rather than buying cheap, flimsy screens, so that mosquitoes and flies can't attack you or your pets and spread disease inside your home. Once you have good screens in place, keep in mind that the air you let in from outdoors needs help circulating around your home, so use a powerful fan to help move the air. Keep the blades clean and free of dust so that those dust particles, along with any mites they harbor, won't be set into orbit in your home atmosphere.

Outdoor air has its challenges: As outdoor air fills your home, it can also bring with it additional dust, pollen, and other environmental matter that could cause an allergic reaction in people and pets. Plus, the sad state of pollution in the world today means that the air you let in through an open window carries with it many other undesirable particles, including dust, mites, bacteria, mildew, and mold.

Now add to all that the particulate matter that comes off our cats and dogs, who contribute to indoor air pollution as follows: While self-grooming, animals lick themselves, and their dried saliva is released into the air along with any shedded hair, or on its own as small particles. Some of these particles are microscopic, so they remain suspended in the air.

Just as you remove stains from fabrics with a liquid extractor product, you can remove a range of unwanted particles from your home atmosphere in a couple of different ways. An air purifier will help clean up all that dirty air. With many styles of air purifier available on the market, there's no reason such a machine should detract from your home's aesthetic atmosphere. Besides having a pet species for a name, ultraquiet HEPA air purifiers by RabbitAir look unobtrusive while keeping your air quality up to sniff: the perfect gadget for a pretty, pet-friendly residence. The Henry air purifier by Swizz-Style, on the other hand, looks like sleek modern sculpture. For an even more petite purifier to tackle a smaller space, such as a closet, check out the Brethe Air Revitalizer by Homedics. Also investigate using a furnace filter to help remove particulate matter from the indoor air.

My dog Sam always looks forward to long afternoons spent sunning himself on the deck of my country cottage, with me on the other side of the kitchen's sliding screen door, ready to let him in when he's done roasting. One day, however, he let himself in by clawing his way unceremoniously through the screen, ripping it practically in half. Fortunately, now screens don't need to risk damage thanks to the Gateway Pet Screen Door, a lightweight plastic frame that attaches to the screen, providing an opening for Sam to let himself in or out.

FOR THE BIRDS

Air is the natural element of birds, so any discussion of clean air in a pet residence would be incomplete without considering the needs of winged creatures. Although I knew that birds had strict clean-air requirements, the point wasn't fully driven home for me until Eileen McCarthy of Midwest Avian Adoption and Rescue Services (MAARS) reminded me of the historical use of canaries in coal mines. "If it's not good for birds, it's not good for you," Eileen explains. "Their respiratory systems are so efficient and so sensitive, because of the demands

Eleanor Mondale and her Umbrella Cockatoo, Sarah Beatrice, catch a breath of fresh air outside their Minnesota home; the beautiful Sarah Beatrice was adopted from Midwest Avian Adoption and Rescue Services (MAARS).

of flight, that what can do damage to us or to a dog or cat is going to do a hundred times more damage to a bird. That's the reason they used canaries in coal mines—if the canary fell off its perch, that meant it was high time to get the people out of there. Birds are still sentinels when it comes to air pollution."

Your castle is your bird's nest. He's very far from his natural habitat—the humid rainforest, where the atmosphere is free of toxins—so homes with birds in residence owe it to their feathered friends to take every precaution to make the environment safe for winged creatures' notoriously sensitive respiratory systems. But whether or not we live with birds, we'd be wise to take a page from the bird owners' book, as those precautions will ensure cleaner, safer air quality for us all—especially those of us who are chemical-sensitive.

Here are some steps you can take to thoroughly clear the air in your home. And if you need more incentive, keep in mind that implementing these lifestyle adjustments will help your own lungs operate at peak performance, like a bird's.

- Avoid anything that aerosolizes (in other words, that is propelled into the air), as it's harmful and potentially fatal to birds. Aerosolization can happen several different ways: through heat (as with a scented candle, plug-in fragrance, or "air freshener" diffuser);

Clearing the Air

through steam (as with steam-cleaning carpets); or through outgassing (as with upholstered furniture or carpeting that has been treated with chemicals to resist stains and odor). So never use scented candles of any kind, and when you buy new furniture or carpeting, arrange to have it unpacked and let it sit, uncovered and rolled loosely, in a warehouse or garage for two to four weeks so that it can outgas that "new carpet smell." Even if you can't detect the scent, your bird certainly can and is put at risk. And don't have furnishings professionally steam-cleaned, as the process aerosolizes the chemicals impregnated in the upholstery fabric and/or carpeting. There have been cases where birds have died after their homes were steam-cleaned.

- Don't install vinyl floors in your bird's home; they, too, outgas harmful fumes that you might not smell, but your bird definitely does. Choose linoleum instead (for more about the natural virtues of linoleum, see chapter 1). If you opt for carpeting, choose a low-pile style, as birds view shag carpeting as an enormous toy to pull on and tear up. Sisal or sea grass carpeting is fine; just make sure they're not dyed.

- If you make chew toys for your parrot out of sisal rope, wash the rope first to remove traces of harmful petrochemicals, even if the package says the rope is untreated. Just don't put the rope in the washing machine, as it will cause it to clog. Soak it in the bathtub with nontoxic soap, then rinse, soak, and rinse again; hang to dry. Use only nontoxic cleaning supplies with a pump spray, never caustic cleaners in an aerosol can. Even with nontoxic cleaners, select unscented "free and clear" ones.

- Home renovations can kill birds, because they create a lot of sawdust, and birds can't expel particulate matter by coughing or sneezing as mammals can. Never refinish a wood floor or install flooring with a bird in residence; board the bird with a vet or for the duration of renovation, and bring him back only after your place has been fully cleaned of particulate matter.

- Birds cannot handle mold spores, so if you have a decorative fountain that's aerated, here is your incentive to keep it clean: If you don't, it will release mold spores into the air that will harm your feathered friend. It's the same deal with humidifiers, air conditioners, and vacuum cleaners. If they're not kept clean, they will aerosolize mold, bacterial, and/or fungal particles, polluting your bird's airspace.

- Strong aromas and birds don't mix, and just because a fragrance is natural doesn't make it okay. Chapter 7 discussed the many virtues of lavender oil, but this essential oil's strong scent makes it a no-no in a home with birds (peppermint and tea tree oil are also off-limits). Likewise, just say no to cedar in any shape or form, whether it's cedar hangers in the closet or a Lane cedar chest.

EAU DE TOILET

To leave the toilet lid up, or not to—that's a question discussed in chapter 9. But if you share your living space with other humans in addition to pets, there are times when a quick hit of fragrance is needed to mask the rank odor of human elimination. My favorite way to freshen the toilet water is with rose water that I buy at the supermarket. Once this lovely, natural scent is flushed away, I don't have to worry that I've introduced toxic chemicals into the toilet bowl—it's a food ingredient, after all—so if my dogs decide to take a drink in the loo, they won't be harmed.

On the subject of unpleasant odors, I have hated the smell of mothballs since childhood, when one of my schoolmates would come to class reeking of them. And now that I know their main ingredient is naphthalene, which is a possible carcinogen that's also very flammable, I'm glad I've always been disinclined to go near them. Now imagine how much pets—whose keen olfactory powers are legendary—hate living in a mothball-scented home! To prevent moths from eating your clothing, simply substitute mothballs with natural moth repellents such as cedar or a blend of natural essential oils plus margosa oil and sandalwood powder. (If you live with birds, however, avoid aromatic cedar and essential oils.)

Our pets have exquisitely sensitive noses, so if you're in the habit of using a very strong home or personal fragrance, you'll notice them sneezing from what they perceive as an olfactory assault. No smell at all is much preferable, from their viewpoint, to a powerful perfume. It's important to realize that clean smells like nothing, so before you introduce scent into your pet residence, first be sure that the place is odor-free. Whatever form it takes—cleaning products, room spray, candles, incense, essential oil—perfume is icing on the cake. The "cake" is an unscented home. Only when a place doesn't smell at all should you begin to think about perfuming it. Think about it: You wouldn't spritz eau de cologne on yourself without taking a shower or bath first, right?

Adding a Hint of Scent

Once you've removed offending odors and ventilated and/or filtered your space, it's time to consider adding a bit of atmospheric flourish (unless, of course, you have birds, in which case skip this section and the next). Even if you're not wild about fragrance, a well-chosen one can make visitors to your home feel warmly welcome. Fragrance is often used to establish a welcoming atmosphere. Real-estate wisdom holds that if you're selling a house, it's a good idea to bake an apple pie because the comforting scents of cinnamon, allspice, and yeast conspire to make potential buyers feel so at home that they don't want to leave. Sold!

On that note, I'll never forget the first time I smelled Cinnabon cinnamon buns. It was at McCarran Airport in Las Vegas, I was on my way home from a *Travel & Leisure* assignment, and the heady scent of baking enveloped me. I clearly recall heading toward the source of that aroma like one of the zombies from *Night of the Living Dead*—I just had to have one. (Years later, I learned that the intoxicating fragrance was totally artificial, pumped throughout the airport to make hungry, homesick, impressionable travelers do exactly what I'd done. Duh!)

Fragrance is powerful indeed, so a little goes a long way. In chapter 7, I talked about the cleaning power of lavender essential oil, but lavender oil (or *Lavandula officinalis*) is an all-around delicious scent. I have yet to meet the person, male or female, who doesn't think lavender smells lovely. Another popular—and unisex—natural fragrance is patchouli (*Pogostemon cablin*), which, in addition to having an earthy, musky aroma, also happens to be a natural insect deterrent.

If, like me, you enjoy a subtle wafting of fragrance through your home, and you don't live with birds, simply dab lavender or patchouli oil on your lightbulbs. When the bulb heats up, it will diffuse the fragrance nicely. At the start of summer, when I clean my air-conditioner filters to remove dust and hair, I always add a few drops of patchouli right on the filter. As the air conditioner operates, it sends a gentle breeze of scent through the air that's especially revivifying when the outside temperature climbs into the 90s. Of course, if I lived with birds, I wouldn't be allowed to do this either, as patchouli is a very strong aroma—but my dogs and cats don't seem to mind.

Going Very Fragrant: What's That Smell?

There are occasions that call for a stronger dose of home fragrance (again, provided you don't have birds, who don't tolerate fragrance). Let's say there has just been a spectacular accident, such as an incident of indoor projectile pooping, and you want to make the olfactory evidence go away right now. Keep smudge wands on hand. These are bundles of sage, cedar, and sweetgrass, tied with thin cotton thread, that seem hippie-dippie, but lighting one and waving it around for a few minutes works well to combat nasty odors—and according to Native American tradition, burning them (the process of "smudging") also purifies a home's spiritual atmosphere. According to tradition, if there's been a recent death in your animal family, it's a good idea to smudge as soon as possible afterward, to cleanse the place of sickness and sad energy.

Around the holidays, scented candles come in handy, adding instant festive atmosphere—plus the drama of a dancing flame—to an interior. Obviously, you don't want to leave any burning candle unattended in a home with pets, or tragedy could result. But here's a precaution that's much less obvious: Pet residences should not burn paraffin candles—and most candles

Flopsy Fragrance

Rabbit lovers Kevin Dresser and Kate Johnson, whom I introduced in chapter 1, were inspired by their bunny Roebling's two favorite snack foods—apple and lettuce—to develop apple- and lettuce-scented room sprays. They collaborated on the project with master perfumer Christopher Brosius, who had previously managed to capture and bottle such unusual fragrances as Dirt, Sugar Cookie, Poison Ivy, and—my personal favorite—Tomato. The latter remains one of the best quick-fix weapons against foul-smelling interiors, whether it's a stuffy station wagon or a pair of man-sized, malodorous sneakers.

out there on the market contain paraffin. Have you ever noticed the dark smoke emanating from a fragranced candle? I did, back when I constantly burned very expensive designer paraffin candles when company came over. Then I learned that paraffin is a by-product of the petroleum industry, and that the burnoff is toxic and quite irritating to creatures, both human and animal, especially those with sensitive pipes.

So, for my own and my beloved pets' safety, I threw out all my paraffin candles and switched to eco-friendly soy candles, which burn cleanly and come in decorative containers. Plus, they come in wonderful fragrances—especially the Ergo brand, which offers a pine-scented candle called "O Christmas Tree" that smells every bit as good as a real Tannenbaum. For tapers to insert in candle sticks, I use old-fashioned beeswax ones that I buy at my local farmer's market, from (surprise) the same suppliers that sell honey.

THINK INSIDE THE (LITTER) BOX

When I first began rescuing cats, I used old-fashioned clay litter. What a mistake that was: Not only is clay outrageously unkind to the environment, sitting in landfills without biodegrading, but it also gives off a fine dust that quickly fills the air of your home like a gray fog, and seriously irritates the lungs of people and pets. I promptly switched from clay to litter brands made of corn and wheat, which are dust-free. I've had friends over who thought they were horribly allergic to cats, yet at my place they didn't experience so much as a single sniffle. Many times, people think they are allergic to cats when in reality it's the dust from old-school cat litter that clogs up their sinuses.

Some cats extrude poop that's silent but "deadly." My piano instructor told me she'd consulted her vet about what she might do about the astoundingly malodorous droppings deposited by her cat, Toyota. The vet recommended avoiding any food containing fish; she did that, and it didn't help. So she consulted me, and I prescribed switching litter brands to Green Tea Leaves, which, as its name suggests, is made with green tea leaves. This tea is a natural odor-buster thanks to the enzyme catechin. Many people reserve the leftover leaves from their green tea and scatter them in the litter box for precisely this reason. Of course, the green tea in Green Tea Leaves is a lot more highly concentrated than beverage leftovers, so they're much more effective at absorbing raunchy kitty odor. I'm pleased to report that Toyota's problem was immediately resolved, and she still lives happily with the pianist.

If your dogs and cats share living space, and you use a litter that's made of a natural grain, such as corn, your dog will take every opportunity to help himself to your cat's droppings, which he sees as a free supply of corn dogs. (I know: yecch.) It took me a while to catch on that my border collie, Sheba, was indulging herself like this. She packed on extra pounds— and gave herself fecal urgency, which naturally I had the pleasure of cleaning up. But first I had to smell it, and trust me, few smells are as stomach-churning as twice-extruded cat poop. If dogs eating "kitty caviar" becomes a serious problem in your multispecies household, try using a different type of litter, such as one made of pine, that's less appetizing to canines. Better yet, leave nothing to chance by cutting an access hole into your wall just big enough for a cat to pass through, and small enough to keep out digestively challenged dogs.

Hot-Water Wash

On the subject of cat litter, I've fielded calls on the radio from people whose cats mysteriously began thinking outside the litter box. When I ask what they used to clean the box, they usually say some sort of strong, disinfectant soap or Lysol. That's where they went wrong: As mentioned in chapter 7, the best way to clean a litter box is with hot water, plain and simple. Cats like their boxes clean, but they much prefer a diluted whiff of their own past droppings to the smell of an industrial-strength cleaner. Hot water cleans the boxes nicely, inside and out, and leaves behind just enough cat scent to keep Kitty thinking inside the boxes, and going back to them to do her business. The water in my tap is about 140 degrees Fahrenheit, but if yours isn't as hot and you're concerned about germs, you can boil water on the stove to disinfect the cat boxes.

Many people like to disinfect their cat boxes with chlorine bleach, but I avoid this because, although the bottled bleach one buys at the store is a dilution, chlorine itself is a highly corrosive gas. I don't like to expose myself or my animals to it, even in its dilute form—especially since learning that repeated inhalation of chlorine has done damage to the liver, kidney, blood, heart, and immune and respiratory systems of laboratory animals.

If the hot-water method described above just doesn't sound powerful enough for you, rinse out cat boxes with white vinegar followed by hot water. Or mix up your own powerful cleaner right in each box, using equal amounts of baking soda, unscented dishwashing liquid, and vinegar (add the vinegar last). As this concoction bubbles up, swish it around in the box, then rinse thoroughly with hot water. The sparkling result ought to meet your cat's discerning olfactory standards, as well as your own. If, however, Kitty has demonstrated her distaste for a mistakenly fragranced box, simply recycle that box and get a new one that you clean out only with hot water.

Good Neighbor Policy

If you live in an apartment building, consider adding air freshener to the hallway to keep things smelling fresh—especially on a rainy day. Cat litter really reeks on wet, humid days, whether it's mild outside and the skies are pouring spring showers, or it's freezing and the ground is covered with winter snow. So on those days, since everyone in my building knows about my predilection for pets, I like to spritz a little something on the hallway carpet outside my apartment to prevent anyone from complaining to the landlord.

I don't mean to sound obsessive, but here's a word to the wise: If you have more than one cat, it pays to keep an eye on weather reports and to keep an extra supply of cat litter on hand. The litter in your cats' pans may be just fine one day, but if you're caught unprepared for rain the very next day, it could totally poop out, leaving you in the lurch for litter—and with a big, nasty odor problem on your hands that requires immediate damage control.

THEY THANK YOU FOR NOT SMOKING

Finally, the simplest, most low-tech yet impactful way to clear the air at your pet residence is not to smoke, and to insist that your guests refrain from smoking in your home. There's ample evidence to suggest that secondhand cigarette smoke can cause cancer in companion animals. As if the risks to one's own health weren't compelling enough to make smokers quit, these scientific findings ought to make pet lovers sit up and take notice. A study published in the *American Journal of Epidemiology* found that dogs in smoking households had a 60 percent greater risk of lung cancer; a different study published in the same journal showed that long-nosed dogs, such as collies or greyhounds, were twice as likely to develop nasal cancer if they lived with smokers.

And in yet another study, vets from Tufts University found that cats whose owners smoked were three times as likely to develop lymphoma, the most common feline cancer. Our furry friends don't just inhale smoke; the smoke particles are trapped in their fur and ingested when they groom themselves with their tongues. It takes a lot of discipline to quit smoking—but like all the other things we do to improve the atmosphere we share with our beloved pets, from decorating to cleaning, it's hugely rewarding.

9

Home Safe Home

Going back as far as ancient times, it was quite common to see Bᴇᴡᴀʀᴇ ᴏꜰ Dᴏɢ signs posted outside pet residences, whether they took the form of an elaborate tile mosaic or a simple, hand-lettered wood plank. Nowadays, Bᴇᴡᴀʀᴇ ᴏꜰ Dᴏɢ signs are quaint collectibles (see chapter 2), and it's much more common to see Dᴏɢ Xɪɴɢ or Cᴀᴛ Xɪɴɢ signs-- even Hᴏʀꜱᴇ Xɪɴɢ, Rᴀʙʙɪᴛ Xɪɴɢ, and Cʜɪᴄᴋᴇɴ Xɪɴɢ signs!

We've made tremendous progress: instead of viewing dogs as intimidating home-security devices, we're looking out for their safety and that of all our beloved companion animals. We are our pets' personal security guardians, not vice versa. The extremely safety-conscious among us even hook up webcams so that we can monitor pets when we're away from home.

And yet, so much can go wrong, so suddenly. One of the hardest lessons of Hurricane Katrina was recognizing the importance of alerting rescue workers to the existence of house pets trapped in abandoned or evacuated houses. A window-cling or a sticker on the door, describing the number and type of pets inside, can be a lifesaver in the event a disaster prevents you from coming home or otherwise separates you and your pet. This may seem like a small detail, but

it's a critical one that could mean the difference between recovering your pets and never seeing them again. Opportunities abound for pet residences to address details like this—details that, once planned for, enable you to sit back and enjoy life at home with your animal friends knowing you've taken every pet precaution you could humanly take.

THE HAZARDS OF HOME FURNISHINGS

Looking at the average American home, who would ever think it has the potential to harbor serious pet hazards? But under certain circumstances, some of the most common aspects of a house or apartment can kill or cause serious injury to pets.

The centerpiece of most living areas, the sofa, can be a comfy lounging place for some dogs—or a perilously high platform from which they take a dangerous dive. Breeds with short legs and long backs, such as Dachshunds, Basset Hounds, and Corgis, can become paralyzed by jumping off or on the sofa at the wrong angle. These breeds require help accessing the coziest seats in the house, so please provide them with a leg-up in the form of a ramp or small set of carpeted stairs. These are widely available, in all sorts of materials and styles, and at many price points.

Insurance for Your Furniture (and Other Valuables)

When considering the subject of safety, we need to address preserving the longevity of your belongings as well as looking out for the safety of your pets. Of course, the pets' safety should always take priority. But taking a few simple precautions means you can have the best of both worlds: a safe, pet-friendly home that doesn't sacrifice style, as well as a pet residence where your prized possessions are also safe from harm. The most important concept in achieving this goal is furniture insurance. There are just a few key items you'll need to buy to ensure that your pet residence is covered by an "all-risks policy." Don't worry, though: The items in question, though priceless, are inexpensive.

- **Toys**   Dogs gotta chew, cats gotta scratch—get used to it. (Sometimes cats gotta chew, too.) Keep a few different chew toys on hand so Spot doesn't suffer chew-toy fatigue, and at least one high-quality cat scratcher (preferably two). Toys for big dogs can pose a tripping hazard for humans, however, so try to keep those corralled in a toy chest when they're not in use. See the "Toys: The Prettiest Playthings" section for more on safe toys with style.

- **Nail clippers**   These are necessary to minimize scratches on floors, walls, and furnishings. If your large dog walks on concrete every day, the action of walking will keep his nails filed down. If he's so small that he's usually carried, or so old that he rarely exercises, he'll need "paw-dicure" help from you, a vet, or a groomer. Cats especially need to have the stiletto-sharp tips of their nails blunted with a quick snip, as these leave scratch marks on wood surfaces and puncture marks on fabrics. Please do not have your cat surgically declawed just to preserve your furniture—this is a cruel, outdated procedure that is actually outlawed in England and Italy.

- **A puppy gate**   While housetraining a young pup, it helps to be able to cordon off certain areas of your home, limiting the young'un's access to places where he might get himself into trouble.

■ **Slipcovers** A protective barrier for your upholstered furniture will provide you with real peace of mind, especially if the covers are fabricated out of a high-performance material such as Crypton (for more on performance fabrics, see chapter 3).

A popular pastime among pet lovers is collecting vintage animal figurines that remind us of our own beloved pets, whether they are dogs, cats, birds, or rabbits. Poodles happen to be a very popular collectible; just ask art consultant Barbara Guggenheim, author of *Decorating on eBay*, who collects them for poodle-loving friends. The most finely rendered and highly coveted species of K9 collectible are MIJ, which stands for "Made in Japan" in the post-war period. Breed-specific collectibles also make extra-thoughtful birthday and holiday gifts for dog lovers on your list. If a friend adores Scottish Terriers, for instance, type the word "Scottie" into the eBay search field, and you'll pull up plenty of gift options to choose from.

But these collectibles are as fragile as they are adorable; chip one, as I recently did, and you'll kick yourself for weeks. These things have a way of chipping if you so much as sneeze, or if your dog wags his tail! It is possible to have real pets and ceramic ones, provided you protect the latter from damage. If you don't have cats, it's fine to display breakable collectibles on a high

Pity for Kitty

Sadly, many cats are surrendered at animal shelters "because we're having a baby." Once surrendered, those cats face an uncertain future at best—and most of them wind up put to sleep, especially the older ones. This is a shame, as simple precautions can be taken for infants and cats to live together happily and safely. I am vehemently opposed to the surgical declawing of cats; it's an inhumane procedure that's been outlawed in England and Italy. Simply keeping a cat's nails clipped short with regular "paw-dicures" is a fine safety measure. But if you still fear that your cat will accidentally scratch your baby, try Soft Paws claw covers. Cats get used to them pretty quickly.

If you introduce a new puppy to a couple of preexisting curious cats, consider installing your puppy gate high a few inches off the ground, so that the pup can't squeeze through, but the kitties' all-access passes to your home won't be restricted.

Laying around on the floor, a pet's toys become part of your home décor. Fortunately, it's easy to find safe, good-looking toys that aren't eyesores in a high-style interior. In fact, some of them—such as anything made by Planet Dog—are positively pretty.

shelf; but if you share your home with felines, ain't no shelf high enough. Display your breakables in a glass-fronted cabinet so you can enjoy looking at them and they're safe from harm.

Construction Precautions

If you plan to undertake a renovation project at your pet residence, please look out for the safety of pets at all times. Do not expect contractors and other tradespeople to have your

pets' safety top of mind—that's your responsibility and no one else's. Remember that accidents can happen in the best of families. Probably the most infamous incident of irresponsible pet-residence renovation occurred when Bill and Hillary Clinton moved from the White House to New York's Westchester County. Buddy, the Clintons' famous chocolate Lab, ran out of the house while it was being renovated (someone had carelessly left the front door ajar) and was promptly killed by a passing car.

Sadly, the safety of the former First Dog was nobody's top priority. But you can make your pets' safety priority one by closing dogs and cats in a locked room, so they can't get into trouble exploring things they shouldn't, such as whirring power tools, electric cords, and driveways blocked by heavy machinery. Birds should not be exposed to construction dust, so for maximum safety, it's best to board them with your veterinarian or have friends look after them at their place.

TOYS: THE PRETTIEST PLAYTHINGS

Your animal's toys are much more than pet playthings; gainfully occupying paws, jaws, and claws, they are a valuable form of furniture insurance that help prolong the life of your belongings. Plus, laying around the house, pet toys become part of the furniture. So besides being safe for animals to enjoy, they should (ideally) look attractive enough not to become eyesores.

Any form of preserved livestock part is neither pretty nor pet-friendly: Rawhide poses a choking hazard to dogs, while ears and hooves are preserved with nitrates that can give sensitive dogs a terrible allergic reaction, complete with horror-movie hives. Here, however, are a few safe toys that earn the *Pretty Pet-Friendly* paws-up:

- Planet Dog Orbee-Tuff
- Kong—for dogs, cats, birds, ferrets, and horses!
- Busy Buddy Squirrel
- West Paw Design Huck
- Tuffzilla Ultimate Dinosaur dog toy
- Bodhi Lucky Carp and Lotus Blossom
- Wagwear flavored dog bone
- Nylabone Cheeky Squeaky
- Castor & Pollux vegetable-shaped catnip toys
- DuckyWorld Sour Puss Lemon catnip toy
- Branch, Claw, and Nap cardboard scratchers by Everyday Studio
- Any item of cardboard kitty furniture by Marmalade Pet Care

With its removable top and bottom, Philippe Starck's plastic Prince Aha stool offers high-style, budget-friendly storage for pretty pet playthings and conceals them from view if they're not pretty to your eyes. I call it my haute dog toy chest.

Pets need and deserve lots of toys, but those toys must be corralled or—no kidding—they could cause a human to slip and fall. Toys for big dogs pose the biggest tripping hazard. Worse still, an errant pet toy could be mistaken by a child and, for that one second when Mom isn't looking, could become a "bone of contention" that could lead to an accidental bite. Keep dog and cat toys in a toy chest when you're not there to supervise their use.

Paper Pushers

If you have a pet rabbit or a pair, you know that they love nibbling on everything, so provide them with plenty of cardboard so they can safely chew to their hearts' content. Instead of simply flattening and recycling any corrugated cardboard boxes that come your way, why not transform them into an inexpensive, nontoxic chew toy? Designers Kevin Dresser and Kate Johnson use box cutters to carve holes into corrugated cardboard boxes, creating "rabbit cabanas" for their bunny, Roebling, who proceeds to customize each cabana like an industrious modernist sculptor, enlarging the holes to create more abstract, biomorphic shapes.

OTHER HIDDEN DANGERS

Sometimes, it seems that toxic substances lurk everywhere, lying in wait to harm our best friends. Here's a primer on poisonous substances to keep far away from Spot. Additional hidden dangers are discussed in the following sections.

- **Over-the-counter medication for people** One Aleve, Advil, or Tylenol can kill a dog from intestinal bleeding, so please store painkillers on the highest shelf, out of the reach of inquisitive, investigative pups.

- **Grapes and raisins** Take care not to let your pet have any cereal, pastry, or other food containing grapes or raisins, as they cause kidney failure. And please instruct kids, who love snacking on raisins, never to share their treats with Spot.

- **Xylitol** This artificial sweetener is a key ingredient of sugarless chewing gum as well as many toothpaste brands, and it's poisonous to dogs. So take care not to let your dog pick up wads of chewed gum off the street, and never use human toothpaste on your dog. Also, certain pups mistake your toothpaste tube as a chew toy, so don't leave it within Spot's reach.

- **Pesticides** Understandably, we like to defend our homes against marauding insects, but the pesticides used by exterminators are a leading cause of accidental pet poisoning. Happily, there's an over-the-counter, nontoxic alternative that really works to combat roaches, ants, and flying pests. EcoSmart contains oils of wintergreen and cinnamon and smells good enough to double as an air freshener.

- **Cut flowers** These are grown with toxic fertilizers, which leach out into the vase water, so don't let Spot drink water that's had flower stems standing in it. The safe alternative is to buy sustainable flowers from your local farmers market.

- **Plastic bags** When grocery shopping, bring your own canvas tote bag instead of bringing home plastic baggage. Not only is this friendlier to the environment, but it also

Dried-Fruit Drama

Certain dogs are compelled to devour foods that are deathly toxic to them. They don't even chew this stuff, they vacuum it up whole—and how much fun could that be? My foster dog DD insisted on clinging to the destructive aspect of her puppyhood well after her first birthday. During her gravity-defying phase, when she taught herself to climb my eight-foot metal kitchen shelves and help herself to whatever caught her fancy, she snagged a bag containing two flourless chocolate cookies from the renowned bakery Payard. Chocolate is deathly toxic to pets, so DD's stunt necessitated an emergency visit to the vet for a stomach pump. But grapes and raisins are also toxic to pets (if ingested, they cause kidney failure), so I was good about keeping the raisin supply out of my dogs' reach. Until, that is, the fateful day when I supplemented my granola and yogurt with some Thompson raisins, spaced out, and forgot to replace the two-cup bag of dried grapes back on the top shelf where it belonged.

Wouldn't you know, DD snatched them in the short time it took me to take two of her senior pack-mates for a quick relief walk. I returned to find the bag on the floor, torn open and diminished by half. Since walking the seniors had taken me longer than I thought it would, there was now no time to make it to the vet before closing. DD's belly needed to be emptied, and fast, so I immediately called the Humane Society of New York, which operates an excellent veterinary clinic, and one of their staff vets kindly told me how to induce DD to vomit. Myself.

Following the vet's instructions, I carefully poured hydrogen peroxide down my little girl's throat in five-cc increments (about a teaspoon at a time). Because DD weighs close to fifty pounds, I did this about twelve times, following with a small amount of seltzer water, before I got the desired result. About fifteen minutes later, poor DD began heaving. I knew this would create a spectacular mess, so I quickly spirited her outside. We barely made it over the threshold when up came gallons of viscous bile resembling raw scrambled eggs, in which floated everything DD had eaten today: her breakfast kibble plus a veritable vineyard of raisins, which by now resembled proper grapes because they'd soaked up whatever fluid was in DD's stomach.

We weren't out of the woods yet. DD started licking her chops again, and up came a second helping of slime, this one resembling gingerbread batter. Cleaning the mess first required scooping the raisins and kibble into the garbage, so some other dog wouldn't vacuum up what DD had just brought up, and suffer the fate DD had just narrowly avoided. Sure, I complained, but I really had no right to: as gross as this exercise was, my little girl was going to be okay. That day, her initials stood for Death Defier—and I resolved to keep all dried fruit in dog-proof glass Ball jars.

makes your interior a safer place for small house pets. I once saw one of my cats get his neck caught in a plastic bag-handle and try, frantically, to outrun the thing. Fortunately, I was there to help, but if I hadn't, he could have easily strangled himself. Lesson learned: The fewer plastic bags, the better! If you do keep them around, cut the handles in half so they don't pose a choking hazard.

- **Yarn** If you or someone you live with enjoys knitting or embroidery as a hobby, take care to secure all yarns (in all sizes, and including fiber contents from wool to cotton to silk), far out of pets' reach. If inquisitive cats, dogs, and bunnies ingest them, they can develop fatal intestinal blockage. It's a terrible way to die and a terrible way to lose a pet.

Toilet Bowls and Reclining Chairs

As discussed in chapter 5, the toilet can be a life-saving watering hole in the event that an emergency locks you out of your home (provided you don't use a bowl sanitizer). A tall dog risks nothing by taking a quaff from a chemical-free toilet, but a small animal such as a ferret, hamster, or lizard can easily drown in the bowl, so residences with small pets should not leave the lid up. To small pets, reclining chairs also pose a serious hazard, easily turning into death traps, so these comfy seats are to be avoided.

Computers and Electrical Wiring

Electrical wires are irresistible to puppies, kittens, and rabbits, who could literally get the shock of their lives by chewing on them. Take care to spray exposed wires and cables with a nontoxic, bitter taste deterrent or, better yet, corral them with an organizational device. Take special care with items such as the chargers for your cellular phone and camera by giving them a stylish housing such as the CableBox by BlueLounge—and don't leave the phone or camera where a dog with a powerful jaw could chomp it. I learned this the hard way while writing this book, when I left my cellular phone unattended and my puppy Lazarus promptly

Great Danes and other giant dog breeds have no problem drinking out of the toilet, provided there's no chemical sanitizer in the bowl, and they obviously run no risk of drowning. Small animals, on the other hand, can die if they fall in, so keep the lid down.

(and permanently) disabled the device with his teeth, necessitating the purchase of a replacement.

Computer users and cats have something important in common: They both share a mouse fixation. How many times have you found your cat reclining on your keyboard or open laptop? Mine do this every chance they get. Protect valuable pieces of office equipment with a clear, hard acrylic cover designed expressly for the purpose of safeguarding data from pouncing kitty paws.

Heart of Glass

If a glass breaks on the floor of your pet residence, be sure to get every last little shard up off the floor so they won't lodge in your pets' paw pads or wind up ingested by them when they lick at the floor. I've found that the best way to do this is with a paper towel dipped in hot water—it picks up tiny glass shards that are invisible to the naked eye. After several passes with hot, wet towels, allow the area to dry, and then deploy the vacuum cleaner.

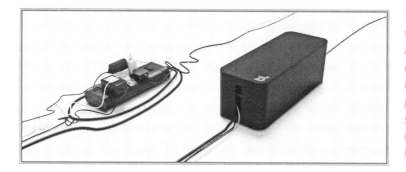

Incidentally, most flower arrangements are made in glass vases, but there now are many high-style options for unbreakable vases. These are made of materials such as silicone and rubber, and they will eliminate broken-vase cleanup. On the other hand, you need to place these soft vases out of reach of certain pups, who might view them as one more pliant plaything to cut their teeth on.

Stormy Weather

When there's no sun up in the sky, many dogs hate to go outside even for a quick relief walk. But for a young, restless dog who requires physical and mental stimulation, the resulting boredom could easily lead to indoor destruction on a grand scale, and Spot could wind up ingesting something quite toxic in his determined quest to entertain himself: Preventing a mishap by turning a rainy day into a day of fun indoor exercise, a pet treadmill is a great way for cooped-up dogs to work up a sweat and tire themselves out without getting soaked, because a properly tired dog is one who won't poke around where he shouldn't.

Cold (Winter) Comfort

The importance of making water available to pets at all times cannot be overstated. Believe it or not, keeping pets hydrated is actually even more critical in winter than in summer. It takes a lot of energy to stay warm in the cold; to do it efficiently, dogs need a continuous supply of water, so please make sure the bowl never stands empty. Here are a few more winter safety tips, courtesy of the Denver Dumb Friends League—because in Colorado, they know cold:

- Don't let snow pile up next to your fence; shovel it away. Even if your dog is not the most agile hurdler, a packed snowdrift will act as a boost, giving Spot just the leg-up he needs to jump over the fence and escape the safety of your yard.

- Antifreeze tastes delicious to dogs, but it's extremely toxic and causes kidney failure. Take care to sidestep those bright-green puddles out on the streets so that Spot doesn't take a poisonous drink or get the stuff on his paw pads, to be licked off later with potentially fatal consequences from kidney failure. If your dog has stepped in antifreeze, give him a paw bath right away. To prevent toxic drip in your own garage, use pet-friendly antifreeze in your car—yes, such a thing exists.

- Keeping a dog's coat well groomed in winter is more than a matter of aesthetics or shedding—Spot may have a thick, glorious, double coat, but if he's matted, his fur won't properly protect him from the cold, so get a good grooming tool and use it regularly. If

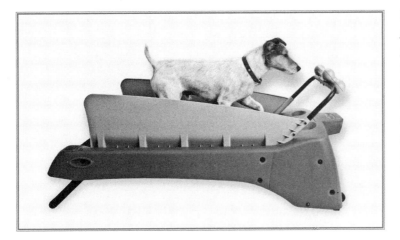

Everyone knows a tired dog is a good dog, but rainy weather prevents active, high-energy dogs from getting their exercise quota. A treadmill is a dogsend that keeps Spot busy, preventing home destruction—and possible serious pet injury—by giving him something fun to do. Spot can do laps while running in place.

Pretty Pet-Friendly

you have a short-coated dog, let him wear a form-fitting thermal layer. Pay no attention to people who think it's stupid to put a sweater or coat on a dog—in cold weather, it's stupid not to.

All Hallow's Hazards

On All Hallow's Eve (a.k.a. Halloween) pets run a greater risk than usual of getting poisoned with chocolate. Make sure your kids and their friends know not to feed chocolate treats to the family pets, and store the Halloween haul high out of reach of inquisitive animals. For the treats you yourself hand out, consider offering costumed kids items that, if swiped by Spot, won't kill him. I like to hand out nonchocolate candies and miniature bags of potato chips and cheese puffs, which offer seasonally correct orange or yellow packaging.

It's also a sad fact that in the days leading up to October 31, many people do heinous things to animals, especially black animals. Some of these people's actions are deeply cruel, and some are meant as harmless pranks, but often the result is the same: The pet suffers. Pets are easily spooked by all the Halloween commotion, what with strange visitors showing up at the door in scary costumes.

If your dog stays in the vicinity of your front door while it's being repeatedly opened for trick-or-treaters, protect Spot from harm and yourself from a lawsuit by making sure that Spot can't slip out the front door, where he may become lost, and that he doesn't pounce on the strangely costumed visitors, believing them to be dangerous intruders requiring eviction. Close cats safely in a bedroom so they can't slip out the front door. In fact, I recommend keeping all pets, especially cats, safe inside in the last two weeks of October.

If you bring the dog along for trick-or-treating, make sure you, the adult, handle the dog at all times. Please take special care not to leave your pet vulnerable to random acts of cruelty at this time of year. If you need compelling incentive, here it is: On October 31, 2007, Halloween night, Bill Whiting of Philadelphia was visiting a friend with his beloved dog, Edna, a small, brown mixed-breed certified as a therapy dog, who went missing during the visit. The friend had opened his door several times to trick-or-treaters, and at some point in the evening, Edna slipped out.

After posting 1,500 lost-dog flyers, ten days later, Whiting received a telephone call from two boys saying they had Edna. Whiting heard the dog's cries and the familiar jangling of her tags in the background. Despite Whiting's pleas and offers of money, one of the boys told him, "Mister, I still want to kill your dog." Five hours later, a boy called to say, "It's dead." Two months later, a suspect was taken into custody: fifteen-year-old Victor Rodriquez. But the teenager was deemed unfit to stand trial, and Edna's body has never been found. This story sickened me to have to report, and I hope it motivates you to keep your pets safe indoors at Halloween time.

Hazard-Free Holidays

Many elements of festive holiday décor can prove deadly to pets. Here are a few Yule rules to keep in mind when decking the halls—and please remember them again at Easter time:

- Avoid glass ornaments, which look like chew toys to curious puppies and kittens; when ingested, they splinter into deadly shards that slice their intestines. If you can't have Christmas without them, hang them on the highest branches.
- Pine trees are grown with fertilizer, which leaches out into the water the tree stands in. Cover the tree so thirsty pets won't drink a toxic chemical quaff.
- If chewed, the cords on holiday lights can electrocute pets.
- Don't use tinsel or "icicles," which can cause fatal intestinal blockage if ingested by curious dogs and cats.
- Plastic Easter grass causes fatal intestinal blockage if eaten.

- Easter Lily plants are toxic to pets; for an Easter centerpiece, consider scattering Easter eggs on a wooden box filled with pet-safe wheatgrass. Pets may safely nibble at wheatgrass to their hearts' content—in fact, it's good for their digestion!

- If you're hosting a party, be sure to assign a trusted adult family member or guest the task of minding the family pet so he or she doesn't run out the door and become lost.

THE GREAT OUTDOORS

As hazardous as the great indoors can be at times, what lurks outside often proves the truth of the line spoken by Lillian Gish in the classic movie *Night of the Hunter:* "It's a hard world for little things."

Bow Wow Does Your Garden Grow?

The yard and garden can pose serious hazards to pets, but pets can also do their share of damage to plantings. Outdoors as well as in, pets need boundaries, and for companion animals and gardens to coexist safely, a few ground rules are in order. If dogs go for your prized plantings, train them by saying "Off!" and reward them with treats when they comply, so they'll be motivated to respect your turf. With cats, lure them where you want them to go by providing convenient patches of rye grass, recommends Rebecca Kolls of TV's *Rebecca's Garden*. "Fill an urn with it, and your cat will curl right up there—that will become her personal outdoor space," Kolls says.

For those areas of your outdoor space where Spot is welcome, exercise caution in your choice of landscaping materials. Avoid pea gravel and small rocks; these can cause choking or intestinal blockage, if swallowed. Dogs love to eat anything chocolatey, including mulch, so don't use cocoa mulch, which contains theobromine, the same toxic ingredient that makes chocolate deadly to pets, and keep Spot away from areas landscaped with it. Cedar is not recommended, as it contains fragrant oils that can irritate pets, causing respiratory or liver problems. Pine bark mulch is the safest choice. Don't plant lilies; if nibbled by a pet, any part of a lily plant, no matter what species, can cause death by kidney failure.

Also avoid chemical pesticides; they are harmful not only to dogs, but also to children. According to Beyond Pesticides, an environmental advocacy group in Washington, D.C., many of the most commonly used backyard pesticides have been linked to cancer, birth defects, asthma, and diabetes. Substitute safe, botanical alternatives such as diatomaceous earth and neem oil (discussed in chapter 5), which is widely used as a soil additive and foliar spray.

Gardening with pets isn't all "don'ts." Do have fun "exterior decorating" by carving out outdoor space for your pets to enjoy. Rebecca Kolls created a path for her black Lab, Winston, that's decorative, dog-friendly, and durable enough to withstand this active dog's daily aerobic romps. To make it, she used shredded bark, mulch, and woolly thyme. "It looks pretty, and it's his very own runway!" Kolls says with a laugh.

Pretty Potty

To keep their lawn green and hygienic, Heather and Kevin Green landscaped a pottying green—that is, a relief area expressly for the comfort of their dogs. Sectioning off the part of the yard dedicated to doo, they had outdoor carpet installers lay down artificial grass over a four-inch-deep sublayer of landscaping material (for drainage). They then trained their dogs to "go" only in the designated potty area, not on the real turf. Three times a week, the area is cleaned with a sprinkler hose, and once a week, it's treated with a nontoxic, biodegradable cleaner.

What Not to Plant

Here's a list of popular but toxic flora to avoid when planting your garden or displaying arrangements indoors:

Pretty Pet-Friendly

Bella the Great Dane takes care of business in the specially landscaped section of her home's backyard. The potty area is covered in artificial turf and hosed clean regularly. This is a smart, attractive solution to the age-old challenge of preventing pet waste from destroying grass.

- Lily (all species)
- Tulip bulbs
- Narcissus bulbs
- Amaryllis
- Crocus
- Azalea
- Rhododendron
- Oleander
- Castor bean

- Cyclamen
- Kalanchoe
- Yew/Japanese Yew
- Chrysanthemum
- English Ivy
- Spathiphyllum
- Pothos
- Sago Palm
- Brunfelsia

The high-style Home Garden by Smeg encases growing things in a decorative "house" of clear acrylic, protecting plants from damage and protecting pets from being harmed by dangerous plants.

Urban Outdoor Hazards

It has been said that city dogs have it better than their country cousins because, well, how many chipmunks and squirrels can a dog chase before boring himself to death? In the city, there are park squirrels to keep a dog connected to his inner predator and a wealth of opportunities to meet new dogs and people—at the dog run, on the street, in your elevator. Urban fire hydrants are portals to the canine internet, a busy place to network, check "pee-mail," and join the discussion by leaving a comment.

Okay, so city dogs don't have to worry about skunks, burrs, and porcupines, but that doesn't mean urban living doesn't have its own peculiar hazards. Dogs can easily bring things home on their paws (or in their mouths) that can spell hours of extra cleanup for you. To appreciate why they call them "mean streets," check out the traps that lie in wait to ruin a city dog owner's day:

- **Snow-melting salt** The stuff used to melt urban ice and snow in winter isn't the same as the salt on your dinner table. It's a chemical so corrosive that it eats away at metal and burns bare paw pads. After an urban outing in the snow, your dog might lift up one paw pitiably, as if he sprained it or has cold feet—but it's really because he stepped in salt and it hurts like hell. Once inside, he'll start licking at his paws to soothe the burning sensation caused by the salt—and that causes digestive upset (translation: vomit and/or diarrhea for you to clean up). Ask your superintendent to replace the existing ice-melter with Safe Paw on your building's threshold, and avoid walking through areas that look freshly melted—seek out patches of snow for Fido to walk in. When you return home, dunk Fido's paws in water to remove anything caustic before he gets a chance to lick it off and make himself sick.

- **Chewing gum**   On hot summer days, city streets become minefields of this molten, gooey stuff. Odds are that your dog will step right in somebody's discarded wad, which is guaranteed to cleave cruelly to the webbing and hair between his toes. Then Spot will begin pitifully trying to lick and/or chew the stuff off. Don't let him—if it's sugarless gum (likely), it contains Xylitol, which is toxic to dogs. Keep a bottle of orange essential oil on hand and use it to remove the gum. If you haven't got orange oil, try one of the kitchen staples suggested in chapter 4.

- **Tree pits**   In the country, trees grow in grassy areas; in the city, they grow in tree pits planted in concrete. And, too often, city dwellers don't respect trees, littering their bases with all manner of detritus, including broken glass, rusty nails, and rat poison. It's not a good idea for Fido to step on and/or lick any of the above, so watch where he puts his paws. If he sustains a cut, don't freak out if he gushes blood; the paw pads are very vascular. When you get home, flush the wounded area with Betadine. If it looks superficial, apply some antibiotic ointment and put a sock on Spot's foot the next time you step out, to keep dirt out of the wound. If the cut looks deep, consult your veterinarian, who will clean and bandage the foot, and possibly prescribe antibiotics.

- **Rats and rodent by-products**   Coming in contact with rodent urine and fecal matter, or the flattened remains of a roadkill rat, can cause a dog to come down with leptospirosis, a serious disease of the liver. If you have a terrier or terrier mix, watch the ground where

Flea Circus

Fleas are a scourge, to be sure, leaving disease, violent itching, and allergic reactions in their wake. But the chemicals used to kill fleas are toxic to pets and people. Let's not shorten our pets' lives while we kill the fleas that plague them! There are effective, nontoxic ways to combat fleas.

If you suspect there are fleas in your garden or under the porch, treat the soil with neem oil, which has been used for centuries to kill fleas dead; you can also scatter nematodes, which are microscopic worms that eat flea larvae.

If you notice fleas on your dog while he's in your home, you'll need to act fast, and it helps to have a cooperative friend or family member to help, as a lot needs to be done on the double. Scatter nontoxic Buck Mountain Herbal Gold Parasite Dust (a mix of neem and diatom flour) wherever you think there might be fleas; allow the powder to sit for a few minutes, and then vacuum thoroughly. If you use a machine with bags, throw out the bag. Bathe your dog with TheraNeem Pet Shampoo, to which you add a tablespoon of straight neem oil. Then throw the towels you just used together with Spot's bedding (and any other washable he may have come in contact with, such as your sheets) in the laundry on hot. Whew—you should be flea-free now.

you walk extra-closely so you can stop Spot from snatching something gross—and be aware that he will pull extra-hard on his leash when he smells a rat, because he's genetically hardwired for hunting rodents.

- **Bones**   In urban areas, these are discarded with abandon all over the street, evidence of fried-chicken or spare-rib lunches enjoyed by hungry urbanites while on-the-go. Your savvy dog is wise to this and views every outing as a strolling smorgasbord. Be on the lookout for bones and be prepared to open Spot's jaw and extract whatever he scores before he can pulverize and swallow it, risking intestinal injury.

- **Restaurant trash**   Some cities have a very high density of restaurants per mile, and that means that on garbage-collecting day giant bags of food—raw as well as cooked—hold the promise of contraband canine treats to the dog actively looking to supplement his diet. If it's the morning after a big night (Friday or Saturday, in particular), the rats will have already started cherry-picking, perforating the garbage bags—and the rat-holes give your dog easy access to leftovers that contain ingredients he's much better off without.

- **Sidewalk cleaning chemicals** The day after a big night, many restaurants—especially those with outdoor tables—instruct their cleanup crews to pour gallons of bleach and other chemicals out on the street. Be careful to sidestep these wet, sudsy areas, as the harsh chemicals could burn your dog's paw pads, causing him to lick and chew at them, which easily results in infection.

Country Culprits

The countryside isn't always the idyllic place it's made out to be. In addition to the very real hazard of coming face to face with a skunk (see chapter 7), a country canine faces a few more possible pitfalls that will require your intervention.

- **Pools** Pools pose a serious drowning hazard to dogs; more than five thousand dogs drown each year in backyard pools, so use a strong cover to close the swimming hole when there's no one on lifeguard duty. For extra safety, outfit water-baby dogs with an immersion alarm that alerts you if your pet falls in the pool.
- **Porcupine quills** Acting in self-defense, an angry porcupine will unleash a torrent of its arrowlike quills all over your dog's face and neck. An infamous photo of a poor dog with his head entirely obscured by hundreds of quills recently circulated all over the Internet (the photo was taken at the vet's office, and the dog is okay). Seek the help of a vet immediately if your dog returns home looking like a pitiful pincushion (and try not to laugh—that's not nice).

- **Flying, stinging insects** I'll never forget the day my poor Sam got bitten by a squadron of angry winged things—to this day, I'm not sure whether they were hornets or just really nasty flies. He was panting miserably, with huge welts popping up all over his body and swelling like a horror-movie special effect. If this should happen to your dog, rush him to the vet, who will administer an injection to combat the allergic reaction.

Pretty Pet-Friendly

Resource Guide

Front cover: 989-103 Lounge Chair by Milo Baughman for Thayer Coggin (available at thayercoggin.com; 336-841-6000) upholstered in Crypton Suede "Icing" (www.cryptonfabric.com; 800-CRYPTON). Tiki, my Chow-Rottweiler cross, adopted from the Delaware Valley Humane Society in Sidney, New York (www.delawarevalleyhumane.org). Kitty, my tuxedo cat, adopted from the Humane Society of New York (www.humanesocietyny.org).

Back cover: Alex "Chair and a Half" by Mitchell Gold + Bob Williams (www.mgbwhome.com; 336-886-4890), upholstered in Polka Dog "Mandarin" by William Wegman for Crypton (www.cryptonfabric.com; 800-CRYPTON). Lupa, my white pit bull (on chair) adopted from the Carrollton Animal Shelter in Carrollton, Texas (972-466-3420); Macska, my white cat, adopted from Ocean County Animal Shelter in Manahawkin, New Jersey (www.fosocas.org); and Angus (on floor) adopted from Animal Care & Control of New York City (www.nycacc.org). Photographed at the living room/lounge I designed for Animal Haven Soho (www.animalhavenshelter.org).

INTRODUCTION

- The **American Dog Magazine:** www.theamericandogmag.com; 303-840-6111.
- **Soles 4 Souls:** www.soles4souls.org; 866-521-SHOE.
- **Locks of Love:** www.locksoflove.org; 888-896-1588.
- **Carlton Hobbs Gallery:** www.carltonhobbs.com; 212-423-9000.

CHAPTER 1

- **Michael Davis Architects:** www.michaeldavisarchitects.com.
- For old-school cat scratchers that stand on the floor, the two pretty pet-friendliest are: **PermaScratch** (www.permascratch.com; 866-713-7292), whose clever design allows you to switch out the vertical scratching surface (a.k.a. "sleeve") when it becomes scratched beyond recognition, which results in a more lasting, less wasteful item of kitty furniture; and **ESmartCat** (www.esmartcat.com; 866-317-6278), whose sisal-covered Ultimate scratching post, with its sturdy, neutral base and top made of light wood, looks right at home in almost any style of décor.
- Here's a simple, inexpensive way to incorporate a **vertical feline scratching area** into your home without taking up extra floor space: Wrap jute or sisal twine tightly around a banister or heating pipe, rub with catnip, and watch Kitty go at it.
- For cat lovers with more contemporary tastes, very high-style, modern **cat furnishings** are available from **The Refined Feline:** www.therefinedfeline.com; 800-289-6136 and Cat Livin: www.catlivin.com; 661-644-8901.
- **Natural-fiber rugs** made of sisal, sea grass, or jute are available at **Crate & Barrel:** www.crateandbarrel.com; 800-967-6696.

- **Iranian carpets selected by Torkan Mahan** are among the most beautiful I've ever seen; Torkan is such a lovely, knowledgeable person that I once named a Persian cat Torkan in her honor: www.torkanusa.com; 212-779-9247.

- **Fashion designer Adrienne Landau's** signature is "easy glamour," and her clothes are worn by animal lovers Halle Berry, Oprah Winfrey, and Julia Roberts, and that high level of glamour infuses Adrienne's home collection as well: www.adriennelandau.com; 212-695-8362.

- **Modular carpet tile by FLOR** is available in many materials and patterns, including my favorite, Coir (coconut fiber), which complements any style of décor; the FLOR tiles used to pave the Brooklyn Bunway are Toy Poodle in Wavy Navy and Babs Blue: www.flor.com; 866-281-3567.

- If you're lucky enough to undertake new construction, **go green** wherever possible for the sake of your pets and the planet; for recommendations of hardwood suppliers and other materials, consult www.buildinggreen.com.

- Working with paint that's tough enough for application to the floor, like paint by **Fine Paints of Europe** (www.finepaintsofeurope.com), necessitates evacuating all pets from the area that's being painted, then allowing the paint to dry completely, and the space to ventilate thoroughly, before letting pets back in.

- **Teragren:** www.teragren.com; 800-929-6333.

- **Artistic Tile:** www.artistictile.com; 877-528-5401.

- **Rubber flooring** is especially kind to senior pets with joint issues; rubber floor tiles by **Johnsonite:** www.johnsonite.com; 800-899-8916.

- **Modwalls:** www.modwalls.com; 877-439-9734.

- **Globus Cork:** www.corkfloor.com; 718-742-7264.

- **National Terrazzo and Mosaic Association:** www.ntma.com; 800-323-9736.

- **Marmoleum** (linoleum floors) by Forbo available in sheet and tile: www.themarmoleumstore.com; 800-842-7839.

- Linoleum flooring also available from **Johnsonite:** www.johnsonite.com; 800-899-8916.

- Vinyl flooring by **Lonseal** offers by far the most intriguing vinyl flooring options; Lonplate, for instance, simulates diamond plate, while Loncoin simulates penny tile; Lonseal also offers the very convincing look of wood grain as well as low-VOC models: www.lonseal. com; 800-832-7111.

- **Wood-grain Plynyl area mat** by Chilewich: www.chilewich.com; 212-679-9204.

- To locate a **feng shui practitioner** in your area, contact the International Feng Shui Guild: www.ifsguild.org; 888-881-4374.

- **Full-spectrum bulbs by Verilux:** www.verilux.com; 800-454-4408.

- The most effective natural brands of cat litter are **World's Best Cat Litter,** made of corn (www.worldsbestcatlitter.com; 877-367-9225); **S'Wheat Scoop,** made of wheat (swheatscoop.com; 800-794-3287); **Feline Pine** (www.naturesearth.com; 800-749-PINE); and **Green Tea Leaves** (www.nextgenpet.com; 949-363-5586).

- It pays to corral newspapers destined for the recycle pile; if you leave them laying about on the floor, they become an invitation to indoor urination, which spells more mess for you to clean. The high-style way to organize yesterday's news is with Willi Glaeser's **Wire Newspaper Rack,** available at the Museum of Modern Art Design Store: www.momastore. org; 212-767-1050.

CHAPTER 2

- **Claw by Everyday Studio:** www.everydaystudio.com; 415-421-1600.

- **Catemporary Cat Tower by The Refined Feline:** www.therefinedfeline.com; 800-289-6136.

- Some of the most beautiful, sweetest pets, from dogs and cats to rabbits and hamsters, are on offer at the beautifully maintained **Massachusetts SPCA Cape Cod Care and Adoption Center:** www.mspca.org; 508-775-0940.

- *Metropolitan Home* subscription information: www.hfmus.com; 800-374-4638.

- Where pet lovers are concerned, **Mythic Paint** is the most important decorative development in the last decade, making it easier for those of us with multiple animal companions to spruce up our homes with completely nontoxic paint that comes in a dazzling array of colors: www.mythicpaint.com; 888-714-9422.

- **FreshAire Paint** offers a much more limited color selection, but is also VOC-free: www.freshairechoice.com; 866-880-0304.

- **Tyler Hall:** www.tyler-hall.com; 212-239-0362.

- *Traditional Home* subscription information: www.traditionalhome.com.

- **Robert Persson** may be reached c/o Heiberg Cummings Design: www.hcd3.com; 212-337-2030.

- **Melissa Barbieri Studio:** www.melissabarbieri.com; 203-622-6975.

- **Demilune cat shelves** constructed for me by master carpenter Christopher Bailey: e-mail baileychris@www.earthlink.net.

- **Catnip** (*Nepatia cataria*) is a species of mint that's native to North America; its active ingredient is nepetalactone, a chemical found in the plant's natural essential oils. Nepetalactone induces an intense yet safe high in kitties that lasts anywhere from a few minutes to ten. Two great resources for organic catnip are **Organikat** (organikat.com) and **Sojo's,** which offers the hand-harvested herb (www.sojos.com; 888-867-6567).

- **Kate Benjamin's blog ModernCat.net** is a must for anyone seeking to live stylishly with cats. Two other excellent feline-design resources are the online home of high-style Brooklynite cat lovers **Bill Hilgendorf and Maria Cristina Rueda** (www.uhurudesign.com) and the website of designer Vanessa von Hessert (www.vonhessert.com).

- **Tabby's Place:** www.tabbysplace.org; 908-237-5300.

- *CRAFT Magazine* **subscription:** www.craftzine.com; 866-368-5652.

- **Porter & Cable** made the **jigsaw** I used to build the Catnip Castle: www.deltaportercable.com; 866-375-6287.

- **Uline:** www.uline.com; 800-958-5463.
- **Pull saw by Shark:** www.sharkcorp.com.
- **Wellness Pure Delights cat treats:** www.wellnesspetfood.com.
- **Spyderco:** www.spyderco.com; 800-525-7770.
- **KatWallks** takes custom orders, so if you have a vintage rug that's the worse for wear, send it along and they will repurpose it as a carpeted cat shelf: www.katwallks.com, 877-644-1615.
- **Everyday Studio** makes two of the most high-style wall-mounted cat scratcher/climbers available, the **Claw and the Branch,** both made of corrugated cardboard: www.everydaystudio.com; 415-421-1600.
- **Marmalade Pet Care's** twist on cardboard, wall-mounted cat furniture is the **Wallflower,** a wavy perch; marmaladepetcare.com; available at www.designpublic.com; 800-506-6541.
- **Scratch n All:** www.scratchnall.com; 888-972-7282.
- **Doyle New York:** www.doylenewyork.com; 212-427-2730.
- **Bonhams:** www.bonhams.com; 212-644-9001.
- **Westminster Kennel Club:** www.westminsterkennelclub.org.
- **Christie's:** www.christies.com.
- **William Secord Gallery:** www.dogpainting.com; 212-249-0075.
- **Hunt Slonem:** www.huntslonem.com.
- **Humane Society of New York:** www.humanesocietyny.com; 212-752-4840.
- **L'Art de Vivre:** 978 Lexington Avenue, New York, NY 10021; 212-734-3510.
- **Carol LeBeaux:** www.silhouettes-by-carol.com.
- **Karl Johnson** creates magnificent large-scale silhouettes of pets and people; www.outarts.com.
- **Jennifer Weinik:** www.jweinik.com.

- **Martha Szabo:** www.marthaszabo.com.
- **Heather LaHaise:** www.heatherlahaise.com.
- **Bettina Werner:** www.Bettina-werner.com.
- **Danger Dogs signs:** www.nepaldog.com; for custom commissions, e-mail photographs to ampage1@gmail.com.
- **Posteritati:** www.posteritati.com; 212-226-2207.
- **Dirk Westphal:** www.dirkwestphal.com.

CHAPTER 3

- To locate **antique curtain tieback** specimens, simply Google those words; one fine resource is www.patternglass.com.
- **Merete curtain panels by IKEA:** www.ikea.com.
- **Pleated paper shades by RediShade:** www.redishade.com; 888-608-6611.
- **Heywood Wakefield:** www.heywoodwakefield.com; 305-858-4240.
- I scored my vintage **Saarinen sofa,** not to mention a **Florence Knoll sofa,** at Brooklyn's famed **The Two Jakes:** www.twojakes.com; 888-2JAKES2.
- New (and more expensive) examples of Saarinen's designs are available from **Knoll:** www.knoll.com; 800-343-5665.
- **Thayer Coggin:** www.thayercoggin.com; 336-841-6000.
- **Surefit Slipcovers:** www.surefit.com; 888-796-0500.
- **Eric Cohler Unleashed** fabric available to the trade from **Lee Jofa:** www.leejofa.com.
- **Carleton V Chiens** fabric available to the trade from **Carleton V:** 212-355-4525.
- **Tyler Hall's "Best in Show," "Adopt Me,"** and **"Cruisin'" fabric:** www.tylerandfriends.com.
- **Adrienne Landau:** www.adriennelandau.com; 212-695-8362.

- **Harry Zarin:** www.harryzarin.com; 212-925-6112.

- **Crypton Super Fabrics**: www.crypton.com; 800-CRYPTON.

- **DogHaus** is the first and only decorator show house to benefit an animal shelter—the **Pennsylvania SPCA:** www.spcadoghaus.org.

- **Barcelona couch** by **Mies van der Rohe** from **Design Within Reach:** www.dwr.com; 800-944-2233.

- **Sheepskin throw from IKEA:** www.ikea.com.

- **Ultrasuede available to the trade from Toray Ultrasuede:** www.ultrasuede.com; 917-342-8486.

- **Ultrasuede accent pillow by Tipsy Starr:** www.tipsystar.com.

- **Seriously sweet dog-themed pillows:** www.pillowpillowpillow.com.

- **Blue Tree:** www.bluetreenyc.com; 212-369-2583.

- **White table from the Conran Shop:** www.conranusa.com; 866-755-9079.

- For any and all upholstery needs, and anything to do with fabric, including vinyl, my go-to resource is **Lore Decorators** (www.loredecorators.com; 212-534-2170); ask for Maria and tell her I sent you.

- **Matelassé bed spreads** available at Restoration Hardware (www.restorationhardware.com) and **Crate & Barrel** (www.crateandbarrel.com); matelassé box spring covers available at Garnet Hill (www.garnethill.com).

- Florida-based **Kris Ogden,** whose catchy handle on www.Etsy.com is "iwoulddyeforyou," is a true **tie-dye artist,** able to enliven anything with brilliant color and make it prettier and pet-friendlier in the process: www.wilddyes.com; 850-862-7237; 850-699-8466.

- **Sunbrella fabric** is designed to withstand anything the weather forecast may bring: www.sunbrella.com; 336-221-2211.

- **Hepper** is a collection of stunning, **ultramodern beds** for cats and small dogs that cleverly eliminates the foam component so many pets love to claw and chew to shreds: www.hepperhome.com; 802-735-0542.

Pretty Pet-Friendly

- **Crypton by William Wegman and Michael Graves:** www.cryptonfabric.com; 800-CRYPTON.

- **Harry Barker dreamy dog beds** are filled with hypoallergenic recycled material and covered with fabric that is azo-free; these beauties are bona fide items of pet furniture, manufactured in America's furniture capital (High Point, NC): www.harrybarker.com; 800-HI-HARRY.

- **West Paw Design beds** are covered in **Polarfleece** made from recycled soda bottles; they are wonderful for short-coated breeds that catch a chill easily: www.westpawdesign.com; 800-443-5567.

- The **removable nylon cover from Fatboy** is just the thing for dogs who frequently get wet; plus it comes in a rainbow of solid colors, plus a Marimekko pattern that was a favorite of Jacqueline Kennedy: fatboyusa.com; also available from www.fetchdog.com; 800-595-0595.

- **Deluxe Pillow Bed with Microban by PetMate**: www.petmate.com; 877-PETMATE.

CHAPTER 4

- For subscriptions to *Elle Décor:* www.hfmus.com; 800-274-4687.

- **Sub-Zero:** www.subzero.com.

- **LG Electronics:** www.lge.com.

- **Smeg:** www.smegusa.com; 866-736-7634.

- As long as we're on the subject of mouthwatering major appliances, let's list the most coveted stoves: **Wolf** (www.wolfappliance.com), **Viking** (www.vikingrange.com), and **La Cornue** (www.lacornue.com).

- *The American Dog Magazine:* www.theamericandogmag.com: 303-840-6111.

- **Master carpenter Christopher Bailey** is a busy man, but he's happy to take orders for custom cabinetry and cat shelves: e-mail baileychris@www.earthlink.net.

- **Open wire shelving by Metro Shelving:** www.metroshelving.us; 866-675-1777.

- **Circular "wood" tiles by Ann Sacks:** www.annsacks.com.

- **Corian:** www2.dupont.com/corian.

- WilsonArt: www.wilsonart.com; 800-433-3222.

- My favorite **vintage light fixture** is a 1970s chrome-and-Lucite specimen by the Italian firm **Sciolari**; I got it at Flessas Antiques: www.flessas.com; 212-289-8484.

- The following are four excellent brands of premium pet food:

    - **Wellness:** www.wellnesspetfood.com; 800-225-0904.

    - **The Honest Kitchen:** www.thehonestkitchen.com; 866-4-DRYRAW.

    - **Blue Buffalo:** www.bluebuff.com; 800-919-2833.

    - **Organix food** for cats and dogs by **Castor & Pollux Pet Works**, www.castorpollux pet.com; 800-875-7518.

    - **Raw beef bones** for dogs available from the butcher at **Whole Foods stores**: wholefoods.com.

- A note on antibiotics and acidophilus: "I believe that pollution, including some chemicals in processed foods and in anti-parasitic applications, as well as environmental pollutants, kill many intestinal bacteria," says Dr. Gerald Buchoff. "If your pet must take these drugs, then it is incumbent on you, the owner, to give probiotics to replace the good bacteria (Lactobacillus, Bifidobacterium, and so on). Just don't give the probiotics at the same time as the antibiotic; give them a couple of hours later." My favorite brand of probiotic capsule is **Jarro-dophilus by Jarrow:** www.jarrow.com; 310-204-6936.

- **Neoplasene** is the plant medicine that has kept my dog Sam cancer-free for two years now, but it is quite controversial; some vets refuse to use it. To locate a holistic veterinarian in your area who has experience treating animals with Neoplasene, contact the medicine's inventor, **Dr. Terry Fox of Buck Mountain Botanicals:** www.buckmountain botanicals.com; 406-232-1185.

- Remove wax, soil, and agricultural chemicals from produce with **Veggie-Wash:** www. veggie-wash.com; 800-451-7096.

- **Colorado Reptile Humane Society:** www.corhs.org; 303-776-2070.

- **Greener Pastures,** which supplies my local New York City farmers market with fresh, organic wheatgrass, will, on request, fabricate simple pine boxes to frame your green stuff: Contact Stuart at 718-852-3979.

- **Walnut Oil by Roland:** www.rolandfood.com; 800-221-4030.

- **Evanger's:** www.evangersdogfood.com; 847-537-0102.

- The **basic training crate is by PrecisionPet,** which also offers an excellent crate training guide. However, if you have a dog who's a champion chewer, be sure to outfit the crate with a metal tray rather than the standard plastic; I've had several dogs protest even temporary confinement by literally eating that plastic tray out from under themselves: www.precisionpet.com; 800-261-3523.

- **PortaPet training crates** are available in both wire and soft models, including one made of my favorite camouflage nylon, plus there's the option of a fitted fleece pad; also available are **PortaTents** and **Portable soft pens** (great for puppy containment): www.portapet.net; 972-342-1346.

- The **eiCrate** is a design coup, its rounded edges a sight for sore human eyes and its rubber liner a dogsend for sore K9 joints; kudos to designer **Peter Pracilio** for pulling off this sleek, chic cage without corners, and for undertaking the design of the corresponding big-dog version still to come: www.designgostudio.com; 347-579-8984.

- Even if your dog is not in danger of bloat, the **DogPause Bowl** is brilliant for multipet homes where one dog eats way faster than her friends. Before I got this bowl, my Lupa would inhale her food, then promptly, and rudely, go poking into the other dogs' bowls; the bowl's partitions slow her down nicely, so everyone may finish munching at (roughly) the same time, and nobody goes hungry: www.dogpausebowl.com; 303-991-1976.

- **Galvanized steel trash cans** in various sizes by **Gilmore-Kramer** (gilmorekramer.com; 800-544-3137). Of course, you probably won't have to store as much dog food at one time as I do, so you can use Harry Barker's gorgeous dog and cat food storage tins, which come with handy metal scoops (www.harrybarker.com; 800-HI-HARRY).

- The **Ball "Ideal" glass storage jar from Jarden** is a giant, four-gallon style that accommodates one seventeen-pound bag of World's Best Cat Litter: www.freshpreserving.com; 800-240-3340.

- **Alessi,** the Italian company world-famous for its haute cutlery and kitchenware, offers **bellissima dinnerware options** for *i gatti e i cani* (cats and dogs to you). The charming **Tigrito** is a cat-shaped resin feeder holding two removable stainless-steel bowls, while the **Lupita** is bone-shaped, with dogs in mind: www.alessi.com.

- **Daisy Dog Studio** makes gorgeous porcelain pet bowls and donates a portion of the proceeds to pit bull rescue, a cause dear to my heart: www.daisydogstudio.com; 646-765-7658.

- For dogs in a great hurry to eat (that describes my almost-always-hungry pups, who feel the service in my kitchen is way too slow), **WetNoz** speeds up the serving process by incorporating a handle in the design of its surgical-grade steel **"Scoop & Serve" bowl,** so it doubles as a handy kibble shovel! Plus, WetNoz makes very high-style feeders that enhance any pet residence: www.wetnoz.com; 888-893-8669.

- **Everyday Studio's clear Plexiglas feeder** is excellent for small spaces that prize contemporary design; although the footprint of the feeder is not small, the clear Plexi gives it an airy, see-through quality that makes a space feel bigger: www.everydaystudio.com.

- For a traditional or country kitchen, **Whiner and Diner** offers lovely **pet feeders** made from repurposed wooden wine crates, with stainless-steel bowl inserts: www.whineranddiner.net; 888-329-8879.

- **Harry Barker ceramic dog bowls:** www.harrybarker.com; 800-HI-HARRY.

- If your pets are delicate and light on their feet (this is code for most cats), by all means indulge in elegant **Rae Dunn Wabi Sabi bowls,** but know that extremely boisterous dogs are liable to put cracks in these in no time; for the aerobic eaters in your pet residence, try sturdy **T&M (Toast and Marmalade) dog bowls** by **Bridgewater Pottery:** both available from www.joannehudson.com; 800-951-1057.

- **The Pet Lounge** offers footed **melamine feeders** for dogs and cats that look like ornate cookie plates from the 1950s, and coordinating trays: www.thepetlounge.com; 603-524-5263.

- **Aquasana water filters:** www.aquasana.com; 866-NO-BOTTLE.

- Since I got turned on to **Healthy Mouth** (www.healthymouth.com), I'm determined that it's the only water my dogs and cats will ever drink: helping pets maintain oral health can add up to five years to their lives, plus drinking dental care is infinitely easier than struggling with pets to brush their teeth!

- Two manufacturers of stylish, sturdy restaurant-style tableware are Hall (hallchina.com; 330-385-2900, ext. 159) and Homer Laughlin (www.homerlaughlin.com; 800-452-4462, menu option #1), makers of the famous Fiesta dinnerware.

- **Naked Sponge by Twist:** www.twistclean.com; 303-443-9953.

- **High-style cellulose sponges** also available from **Casabella:** www.casabella.com; 800-841-4140.

- **Vigorate nourishing dog treats** are the K9 equivalent of the human supplement Juvenon, helping our dogs maintain healthy cell function as they age: www.vigorate.com; 800-588-3666.

- **Platinum Performance** is another excellent company that manufactures supplements for both people and animals: www.platinumperformance.com; 800-553-2400.

- **Nupro** offers a complete line of **nutritional supplements** for dogs and cats: www.nuprosupplements.com; 800-360-3300.

- Made of predigested white fish protein, **SeaCure** helps right a pet's upset stomach safely and naturally, and is a dogsend if your dogs—like mine—frequently supplement their top-notch premium diets by snatching rancid trophies while out for a walk (in other words, this stuff can stop doggie diarrhea in its tracks); it also comes in quite handy if you need to switch foods, whether it's because you ran out of your pet's normal diet or you're upgrading him to a different brand: www.naturedoc.com; 800-952-5884.

- **ArthroPet** joint support supplements **by NeoCell:** www.neocell.com; 800-346-2922.

- **Hawthorn, valerian, lepsilyte, and milk thistle** (as well as many other excellent plant medicines, plus glucosamine sulfate) available by vet prescription from **Buck Mountain Botanicals:** www.buckmountainbotanicals.com; 406-232-1185.

- Learn more about the remarkable healing properties of **Manuka honey:** www.manuka honeyusa.com (be sure to check out Fluffy, the company's adorable K9 mascot!); 720-524-3237.

CHAPTER 5

- **Tomy Maugeri Dog Salon:** www.tomydog.com.

- **Towel** monogrammed with the legend, "The most affectionate animal in the world is a wet dog" from **Mouthfuls:** www.mouthfuls.net; 720-855-7505.

- **One Dog One Bone** pool: www.onedogonebone.com; 602-329-9581.

- **Booster Bath:** www.boosterbath.com; 888-494-4004.

- **Rapid Bath:** www.rapidbathing.com; 877-786-4358.

- Lucky indeed is the dog who gets bathed regularly indoors, in his very own **whirlpool bath.** If I ever get the chance to build my dream bathroom, the main feature will be a **Jentle Pet** 200 by MTI Whirlpools: www.mtiwhirlpools.com; 800-783-TUBS.

- For long-haired dogs who need to follow a bathing with a blowout, the tool to use to make the chore go faster is the **Air Force Quick Draw pet dryer:** www.showeryourpets. com; 877-840-5224.

- **Beverly Hill's LaunderMutt:** 212-691-7700.

- **Sudsy Dog in Lakewood:** www.sudsydogwash.com; 562-377-1360.

- **Furminator:** www.furminator.com; 636-680-9387.

- **Dog Body Brush with Shampoo Applicator by Bamboo:** www.bamboopet.com; 877-224-PETS.

- Towel by **Farfetched:** www.farfetched.com; 707-829-1867.

- **Fur shampoo:** www.furdogsnyc.com; 212-595-6002.

- **Organimals** by Aubrey Organics: www.aubreyorganics.com; 800-282-7394.

- **Vermont Soap Organics Dog Shampoo:** www.vermontsoap.com, 866-762-7482.

- **TheraNeem Pet Shampoo, Neem Oil,** and **Supercritical Extract** supplements from OrganixSouth: www.organixsouth.com; 888-989-NEEM.

- Just how do the creators of **Buddy Wash** stand by their gentle **dog shampoo and conditioner?** Enough to wash their two small kids with it: www.cloudstar.com; 800-361-9079.

- **Tropiclean:** www.tropiclean.net; 542-7387.

- **Spa:** www.spalavishyourpet.com; 800-542-7387.

- **Spa Dog Botanicals:** www.spadogbotanicals.com; 866-674-7770.

- **Sulphur Springs Animal Shelter:** Sulphur Springs, TX; 903-438-9369.

- **Buck Mountain Herbal Gold Parasite Dust:** www.buckmountainbotanicals.com; 406-232-1185.

- **MudMagnet Paw Cleaning Glove by Bamboo:** www.bamboopet.com; 877-224-7387.

- **CasaPet Microfiber Paw Cleaning Mitt** by Casabella: www.casabella.com; 800-841-4140, ext. 184.

- **Gentle Pet Wipes** by Mrs. Meyer's Clean Day: www.mrsmeyers.com; 877-865-1508.

- **Paw Plunger:** www.pawplunger.com.

- **Omega Zapp Skunk Odor Conditioning Shampoo** available at Tails & Company: www.tailsandcompany.com; 877-924-2253.

- **NOW (Nutrition for Optimal Wellness) orange oil**: www.nowfoods.com; 888-669-3663.

- **Angel the Cockatoo** rescued by **Midwest Avian Adoption and Rescue Services:** www.maars.org.

CHAPTER 6

- **Gentle Pet Wipes by Mrs. Meyer's Clean Day:** www.mrsmeyers.com, 877-865-1508.
- **Hand Sanitizer Wipes** by Clean Well are gentle enough to use on pets' paws: www.cleanwelltoday.com; 415-839-6393.
- **Paw Plunger:** www.pawplunger.com.
- Bamboo makes **quality nail clippers for pets:** www.bamboopet.com; 877-224-PETS.
- With its unique filing system and safety feature, the **PediPaws Pet Nail Trimmer** takes the horror out of clipping a pet's nails, and leaves the claws smooth, so they will cause less scratching damage to your floors: www.pedipaws.com; 800-777-4034.
- **Fred Humidifier** by SwizzStyle: www.swizzstyle.com; available at www.productswithstyle.com.
- **Furminator:** www.furminator.com; 636-680-9387.
- **Brush Buddy:** www.thebrushbuddy.com; 888-752-1777.
- **Lawn and Leaf** bags by BioBag are completely biodegradable and compostable, as are BioBag's dog waste bags, cat pan liners, and tall kitchen bags: www.biobagusa.com; 727-789-1646.
- **Dyson:** www.dyson.com; 866-693-9766.
- **Pet Hair Eraser Hand Vacuum** by Bissell: www.bissell.com; 800-237-7691.
- **The Germ-Killing Vacuum** by Halo: www.uv-vacuum.com; 877-879-4256.
- FreshWave offers a complete range of excellent, all-natural cleaning and deodorizing products, including **Vacuum Pearls and Carpet Shake:** www.fresh-wave.com; 800-662-6367.
- **Felix by Sebo:** www.sebo-vacuums.com; 303-792-9181.

- A black light has many uses besides helping find pet stains, including checking antiques, driver's licenses, and currency, and also locating scorpions (!); try the Chauvet six-inch handheld black light with flashlight: www.blacklight.com; 866-316-7311.

- **Odorzout:** www.88stink.com; 800-88STINK.

- **Clear the Air:** www.cleartheair.com; 800-611-1611.

- **Roomba:** www.irobot.com; 800-727-9077.

- **The Maids Home Service:** www.maids.com; 800-THEMAIDS.

- **SaveKitty Foundation:** www.savekitty.org; 347-993-3163.

- **3M Fur Fighter Hair Remover** available at Target (www.target.com) and Wal-Mart (www.walmart.com).

- **Microfiber Chenille Flex Floor Duster** and **Water Stop All-Purpose Gloves** by Casabella: www.casabella.com; 800-841-4140, ext. 184.

- **OXO Good Grips dust pan and brush:** www.oxo.com; 800-545-4411.

- **Pylones dust pan and brush:** www.pylones-usa.com; 800-743-0131.

- **Petmate litter catcher mat** (www.petmate.com; 877-738-6283); you can also make your own fun litter catcher mat out of a square of "Green Acres" by FLOR (www.flor.com; 866-281-3567) or a half-circle of synthetic turf from Perfect Turf (www.perfectturfinc.com; 888-SYN-TURF); the company's Factory Specials selection includes many vibrant colors other than classic green, including high-style lipstick red and lacquer black.

- **Helmac Evercare Pet Hair Pic-Up:** www.helmac.com; 800-435-6223.

- **Sticky Sheets:** www.stickysheets.com; 888-878-4259.

- **Eames Hang-it-All** available at the Museum of Modern Art Design Store: www.momastore.org; 212-767-1050.

- **Harry Barker's charming dog-breed leash racks** take the shape of a Poodle, Lab, or Scottie: www.harrybarker.com; 800-HI-HARRY.

- You can also hang your leashes from Phil Cuttance's Trophy Hanger, with a hook shaped like the head and neck (or, alternately, the rear end!) of a moose, giraffe, or hippo; available at Charles & Marie: www.charlesandmarie.com.

- Yet another witty option for leash storage, provided you don't have more than two lightweight (i.e., nonleather) leashes, is **David Wiseman's charming Everyday Studio's clear Plexiglas feeder** with its sweet shades of Bambi; available from the **Whitney Museum of American Art**: www.whitney.org/store.

- **The Vicci Hygiene Basin** was the world's first high-style litter pan; it blazed the trail that many pet manufacturers now travel: www.unitedpets.com.

- **Cats Rule,** makers of litter boxes in open and closed styles: www.catsrule.com; 954-384-2705.

- **Kitty a Go-Go,** a high-style closed litter box with a slide-out tray: www.kittyagogo.com; 877-548-8946.

- **Hidden Litter** is a litter box that looks like a planter complete with artificial foliage: www.petsbestproducts.com; 800-884-1917.

- **Ultimate Litter Box and Corner Litter Box:** www.esmartcat.com; 866-317-6278.

- **Kattbank:** www.kattbank.com.

- For less expensive (than the pricey Kattbank) items of furniture that also cleverly conceal kitty loos, check out the **Refined Litter Box and Catemporary Cat Box,** both available from **The Refined Feline**: www.therefinedfeline.com; 800-289-6136.

- **BIO-Nesting by NuHemp** is small-animal bedding made of organic hemp; safe to use for rabbits, hamsters, gerbils, mice, rats, ferrets, guinea pigs, and lizards, it's twice as absorbent as conventional small-animal bedding, naturally antimicrobial, and compostable: www.petfooddirect.com, 800-865-1333.

- **CareFresh Pet Bedding,** made of cellulose fiber, available at **Arcata Pet Supplies:** www.arcatapet.com, 800-822-9085.

CHAPTER 7

- **NOW** (Nutrition for Optimal Wellness) **lavender oil and tea tree oil:** www.nowfoods.com; 888-669-3663.

- **Earthworm:** www.acleanearth.com; 888-728-5770.

- **Method Home Wood for Good, Daily Shower** (for tiles and grout), **Home Cucumber** or **Pink Grapefruit All-Surface Cleaner:** www.methodhome.com; 866-9-METHOD.

- **Farmhouse Furniture Wax:** www.farmhousewares.com; 866-567-7958.

- **Ecos Furniture Polish:** www.ecos.com; 800-335-3267.

- **Bamboo Goo:** www.shopbluehouse.com; 877-276-1180.

- No matter now nontoxic the product you're using or how much you dilute your **floor cleaner,** please take care to close pets out of the room while you're mopping, polishing, or otherwise swabbing your decks. Apart from the risk of them licking at the wet surfaces, their paw pads can also absorb the cleaning product, and that's not pet-friendly.

- **National Anti-Vivisection Society:** www.NAVS.org; 800-888-NAVS.

- **Sun & Earth:** www.sunandearth.com; 800-298-7861.

- **Parsley Plus Kleener:** www.ecos.com; 800-335-3267.

- **Ecos Window Kleener:** www.ecos.com; 800-335-3267.

- **Life Tree Products** include Citrus Fresh Dish Soap, Automatic Dishwashing Liquid, Fresh + Natural All Purpose Spray Cleaner, and Fresh + Natural Bathroom Cleaner with Tea Tree and Lavender Oils: www.lifetreeproducts.com; 800-824-6396.

- **Seventh Generation** Free & Clear Natural 2X Concentrate Laundry Liquid, Natural Fabric Softener, and Chlorine-Free Bleach: www.seventhgeneration.com; 800-456-1191.

- **Ecover** Non-Chlorine Bleach: www.ecover.com/us/en; 800-449-4925.

- The prettiest cellulose sponges are by **Casabella,** which helps you prolong the life of your sponge by offering a sponge designed to hook onto your faucet, where it can hang to dry: www.casabella.com; 800-841-4140, ext. 184.

- **Clean Well hand sanitizer with Ingenium** (cleanwelltoday.com) available at Whole Foods stores: www.wholefoods.com.
- **Dr. Gerald Buchoff:** www.holisticpetcarenj.com; 973-256-3899.
- De-stress your pet residence's aural atmosphere with **healing harp music by Susan Raimond:** www.petpause2000.com; 619-473-0241.
- Maintaining as many animals as I do would simply not be possible without **Get Serious,** a serious dogsend: www.getseriousproducts.com; 714-414-1111.
- **Planet Ultra Liquid Laundry Detergent:** www.planetinc.com; 800-858-8449.
- **Vermont Soap Liquid Sunshine:** www.vermontsoap.com; 866-762-7482.
- **Method Home 3X** laundry detergent is an awe-inspiring product in a great, ergonomic package, and it even whitens blackened, filthy white slipcovers. Be very careful not to get it on your skin, however – I did this and the skin on my fingers started turning white, and wouldn't stop stinging even after a thorough rinsing with water. Here's what ultimately stopped the burn: Neem Oil from OrganixSouth (www.organixsouth.com), which has been used for centuries to heal both chemical and temperature burns as well as many skin irritations. The next time you burn yourself ironing or cooking, try it and see!

CHAPTER 8

- For a powerful gust of indoor air, a **Vornado air circulator** is in order: www.vornado.com; 800-234-0604.
- I wish we could purify the atmosphere of the entire world with a gigantic **RabbitAir;** in the meantime, if every pet residence uses one, global air quality ought to improve: www.rabbitair.com; 888-866-8862.
- **Henry Air Purifier by SwizzStyle** (swizzstyle.com) available at the Museum of Modern Art Design Store: www.momastore.org; 212-767-1050.
- **Brethe Air Revitalizer by Homedics:** 800-333-8282.

- The **Best Air pet furnace filter** is designed to cut down on pet dander and allergens: www.rpsproducts.com; 847-683-3400.

- **Gateway Pet Screen Door and Endura Flap** boast a weather-tight seal; available at www.petdoors.com; 800-826-2871.

- **Midwest Avian Adoption and Rescue Services (MAARS):** www.maars.org; 651-275-0568.

- **Rose Water:** www.ahmedfood.com.pk; e-mail afpkltd@cyber.ret.pk; 92-21-257-8196.

- **NOW** (Nutrition for Optimal Wellness) **patchouli oil:** www.nowfoods.com; 888-669-3663.

- **Global Shaman Smudge Sticks** available at **Whole Foods stores:** www.wholefoods.com.

- **Ergo soy candles:** www.ergocandle.com; 214-905-9050.

- **Jimmy Belasco soy candles:** www.jimmybelasco.com; 866-391-2726.

- Brooklyn Bunny's **Apple Room Spray and Perfume** and **Lettuce Room Spray and Perfume:** www.bklynbunny.com.

- For comprehensive information on the care of rescued pet rabbits, consult the **House Rabbit Society:** www.rabbit.org.

- **Green Tea Leaves cat litter:** www.nextgenpet.com; 949-363-5586.

- **Smell Killer by Zielonka;** this German company has devised a range of ingenious products made of metal to eradicate every imaginable odor in your home, including the man of the house's stinky sneakers: www.Zielonka-Shop.com; 704-329-5100.

- Electronic CatMouse effectively targets the source of foul odors known as the cat box: www.InstantFreshAir.com; 262-334-3000.

- **Colibri Anti-Moth Hanging Sachets** (www.colibriantimoth.com) are a pleasantly fragrant, all-natural alternative to mothballs, combating wardrobe-eating insects with a blend of natural essential oils plus margosa oil and sandalwood powder: www.ShopBlueHouse.com; 877-276-1180.

CHAPTER 9

- Charming, hand-painted **"Animal Xing" signs:** www.NepalDog.com.

- **PetCam by Panasonic:** 2Panasonic.com; 800-211-7262.

- **PetCam by Xanboo:** www.Xanboo.com; 212-714-2295.

- To prevent the tragic separation that befell so many people and pets during Hurricane Katrina, **MuttShack Animal Rescue Foundation** offers a free online disaster preparedness course: www.muttshack.org.

- To corral puppies where you can monitor their movements without doing damage to your walls, investigate a stylish, well-made pet gate: three pretty pet-friendly ones are the **Standalone Pet Gate, Push Button Gate,** and **Telescoping Pet Gate:** all available from www.fetchdog.com; 800-595-0595.

- **Soft Paws claw covers:** www.softpaws.com; 800-989-2542.

- Your dog will welcome any toy by **Planet Dog,** especially the fruits and vegetables: www.planetdog.com; 800-381-1516.

- When filled with schmears of peanut butter, cream cheese, and other delectables, the **Kong** is a great babysitter: kongcompany.com.

- **Nylabone's Rhino** and **Premier Pet's Busy Buddy Squirrel Dude** are similar to the Kong, only they come in more fashionable colors, such as purple: nylabone.com; 800-631-2188.

- **West Paw Design** makes colorful, high-performance **interactive toys** that are also recyclable, so you won't feel like a sinner sending nonbiodegradable matter out into the environment: www.westpawdesign.com; 800-443-5567.

- **The Spring Roll dog toy by WetNoz** has a sleek, contemporary silhouette (www.wetnoz.com; 888-893-8669), as does the **TreatStik** (www.treatstick.com; 802-649-8448).

- A menagerie of **dinosaurs and sea creatures** make up the **Tuffies** bestiary, and any of these toys look smashing in a kid's room: www.tuffietoys.com; 866-478-0848.

- **Wagwear's sleek gum rubber bone** comes infused with four irresistible scents (chocolate, cashew, pistachio, or peanut butter): www.wagwear.com; 888-WAGWEAR.

- I know a pretty pit bull named Harpo who plays incredible jazz symphonies on her **Cuz squeaky toy by JW Pet:** www.jwpet.com; 800-407-7826.

- For men who'd prefer that a dog's toys be, well, more manly than pretty, **Hyper Products** has excellent dog toys that take the shape of, for instance, a **hammer and wrench,** a **baseball bat,** and a **soccer ball:** www.hyper-products.com; 866-476-5614.

- **Nylabone** offers **soft Frisbees** for dogs that are very boy: www.nylabone.com; 800-631-2188.

- **Curious Cat Organic Catnip toys by Castor & Pollux Pet Works** take the shape of vegetables and are adorable without being cutesy: www.castorpolluxpet.com; 800-875-7518.

- For more food-inspired toys, check out **Yeowww! Sour Puss Lemon, Yeowww! Apple,** and **Yeowww! Banana by Ducky World:** www.duckyworld.com; 866-493-6999.

- Corrugated **scratcher/loungers** by **Marmalade Pet Care** let felines multitask by engaging simultaneously in the two activities most important to them—stropping their claws and catnapping: www.designpublic.com; 800-506-6541.

- Composed of botanical ingredients such as wintergreen oil and cinnamon oil, **EcoSmart roach and ant killer** is effective at eliminating its targets, yet totally safe to use around children and pets (again, birds are the exception—never spray a product like this in the presence of winged creatures): www.ecosmart.com; 877-723-3545.

- **Prince Aha stool by Philippe Starck for Kartell:** www.unicahome.com; 888-89-UNICA.

- **The CableBox by BlueLounge** offers shelter to wayward cords, preventing tragedy by making it harder for pets to access them: www.bluelounge.com; 626-564-2802.

- **Doug Mockett & Company** commissioned talented designers to tackle the problem of taming wires and cords; **Andrea Ruggerio** devised the **Sombrero wire manager,** and **Harry Allen, the Wirestay:** www.mockett.com; 800-523-1269.

- **Step-ups** are a must to help short-legged, long-spined dogs (like Dachshunds and Basset Hounds) or senior dogs of any breed or mixture to gain access to your home's coziest spots, and prevent them from jumping down and running the very risk of joint injury or permanent paralysis. Solvit's lightweight, durable **Ultralite Pet Stairs** are unobtrusive-looking and strong enough to hold up to 250 pounds: www.solvitproducts.com; 866-6-SOLVIT.

- **Clear acrylic Pet Proof Keyboard Cover** by ViziFlex Computer Solutions: www.viziflex.com; 800-627-7752.

- **Rubber vases by the Belgian company D&M Depot** (www.dmdepot.be) are unbreakable and unimpeachably high-style: www.roseandradish.com; 415-864-4988.

- **PetZen "Dog Tread" treadmill:** www.petzenproducts.com; 877-563-5151.

- **Denver Dumb Friends League:** www.ddfl.org; 303-751-5772.

- **Neem Oil for the Garden available from Organix South:** www.organixsouth.com, 888-989-NEEM.

- No time to go to your local nursery? **Mail-order plants** are available from the following: www.whiteflowerfarm.com; www.heronswood.com; and www.selectseeds.com.

- Not sure whether a plant is pet-friendly? The **ASPCA's Animal Poison Control Hotline** is staffed 24 hours a day, 365 days a year: 888-426-4435.

- **Synthetic Animal Turf for dog runs by Perfect Turf:** www.perfectturfinc.com; 888-SYN-TURF.

- Billing itself as "Your Backyard in a Box," The Pet Loo is an apartment-size patch of turf that drains into a handy tray for pets' indoor-elimination convenience: www.thepetloo.com; 646-383-8886.

- **Home Garden by Smeg:** www.smegusa.com; 866-736-7634.

- **Safe Paw ice melter:** www.safepaw.com; 800-783-7841.

- **Ecos Ice Melt:** www.ecos.com; 800-335-3267.

- There's yet another use for **NOW** (Nutrition for Optimal Wellness) **orange oil:** since cats generally don't love the scent of citrus, rub some into those wood furnishings you'd rather not have scratched, and it will keep the kitties away, thereby protecting the wood while conditioning it: www.nowfoods.com; 888-669-3663.

- **Betadine** is a great thing to keep in your first-aid kit; any time your pets (or you) sustain a cut, simply flush the wound with a dilution of this povidone iodine product to kill bacteria; follow with some Bacitracin or generic antibiotic ointment, and then hightail it to the vet.

- When the need arises to cover a dog's injured paw, instead of a sock, try **Pawse rubber paw-covers, available at The Pet Stop:** www.petstopnyc.com; 212-580-2400.

- **Buck Mountain Herbal Gold Parasite Dust:** www.buckmountainbotanicals.com; 406-232-1185.

- Take care to monitor pets and children around the pool with the **Safety Turtle,** which emits an alarm if someone vulnerable wearing the device falls in: www.safetyturtle.com; 800-368-8121.

- For the maximum security of pets and children, close your pool with a **Loop-Loc Safety Swimming Pool Cover:** www.looploc.com; 800-LOC-LOOP.

- On ordinary days, I refresh the atmosphere in the common hallway of my building with **Fresh Wave Home Spray:** www.fresh-wave.com; 800-662-6367.

- But on those days when it's raining, ahem, cats and dogs, and I want to be sure that no litter box odors affect the air quality in the common hallway of my building, I use **Febreze** out there. Yes, it's an industrial-strength concoction, but in this case it's useful, because people are familiar with it and it says "smells clean" to them. There were rumors that Febreze's parent company, Procter & Gamble, was involved with animal testing, but that's no longer the case; in fact, the ASPCA, America's first humane organization, approves of Febreze for simplifying life with animals and encouraging shelter-pet adoption. Just please remember never to spray Febreze directly on your pets or their bedding, and don't use it at all if you live with birds.

- Your pets would prefer that you don't step on them on a middle-of-the-night trip to the loo; light your way with the ambient LED light of the **rechargeable Candela by OXO,** which offers eight hours of soothing nighttime illumination: www.oxo.com; 800-545-4411. Or check out personalized Pet Night Lights: www.PetNightLights.com; 623-322-2484.

Index

Index